THE COMPLETE GUIDE TO
MACHINE QUILTING

THE COMPLETE GUIDE TO
MACHINE QUILTING

How to Use Your Home Sewing Machine
to Achieve Hand-Quilting Effects

Joanie Zeier Poole

St. Martin's Griffin
New York

THE COMPLETE GUIDE TO MACHINE QUILTING

www.stmartins.com

Library of Congress Cataloging-in-Publication
Data Available Upon Request

ISBN: 978-1-250-00425-3

QUAR.QSM
Conceived, designed, and produced by
Quarto Publishing plc
The Old Brewery
6 Blundell Street
London N7 9BH

Senior editor: Chloe Todd Fordham
Art editor and designer: Julie Francis
Illustrators: John Woodcock, Luise Roberts
Photographers: Phil Wilkins, Simon Pask,
Sian Irvine
Picture research: Sarah Bell
Art director: Caroline Guest
Creative director: Moira Clinch
Publisher: Paul Carslake

Color reproduction by
PICA Digital Pte, Ltd, Singapore
Printed in China by
Hung Hing Printing Group Ltd

First U.S. Edition: May 2012

10 9 8 7 6 5 4 3 2 1

When following the measurements in this
book, choose either metric or imperial
and be consistent throughout.

Contents

Foreword

It is my pleasure to introduce you to machine quilting, a wonderful skill that will help you to complete quilts efficiently and with versatile results. Machine quilting is economical, using equipment you already own to complete your quilts. The projects displayed in this book, as well as my competition quilts (www. heirloomquiltingdesigns.com), were completed using domestic sewing machines. Whether using an old faithful machine that is 45 years old, or a new high-tech model, my success comes from the materials I use, the way I handle the machine, and how I fill the surface with imaginative quilting designs.

This is my classroom in a book, offering you information on the machine quilting process from beginning to end. The art of machine quilting offers challenges that all beginners encounter. These situations are not new, nor are they happening only to you. The good news is that I have gathered what I feel is the most useful information, then added my personal experience to guide you through the mysteries of machine quilting. You will discover information that is vital to making your machine quilting as easy as possible, learn what is within your control, and how to simply adjust to the rest.

A close look at the sewing machine, your partner in this work, will allow you to familiarize yourself with the features and accessories designed to make the job go smoothly. You will learn about planning your project with the purpose of the quilt in mind, and how to make a quilting plan, and you will become familiar with the wide variety of fabrics, thread, and batting available to help you determine the best choice for your project. I put my years of experience to work explaining the various machine quilting techniques available to you, from the first stitch to handling a large quilt bundle.

Finally, you can put all that you have learned into action constructing the projects. Each one was designed using a different technique and materials to allow you to practice your new-found skills. Step-by-step instructions and photos walk you through every detail along the way.

Susan Briscoe has gathered quilts from many talented machine quilters and these are displayed throughout the book. Luise Roberts contributed the quilting designs in the back of the book.

This book has all the information you need to get the same polished effects as the professionals. You have so much to gain, and I want you to have the satisfaction of completing your own quilts, with your own personal style. I tell my students the most important factor in learning anything new is desire, followed closely by a positive attitude.

Wishing you success,

Machine quilting in context

Machine quilting is a versatile art that attracts quilters and crafters from all over the globe.
The next few pages showcase the work of some wonderful quilters whose preferred
method of quilting is by machine.

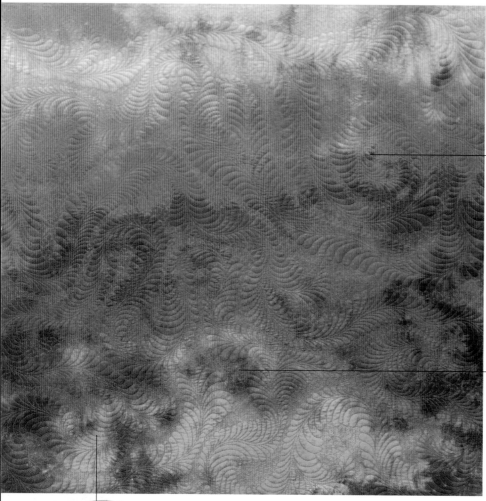

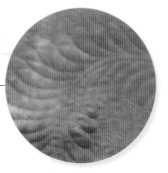

The thread color merges with the fabric
in the top areas of the quilt.

The contrasting thread and
fabric colors at the bottom of
the quilt create a sense
of depth.

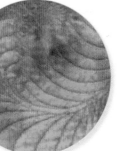

Retraced lines are necessary to create
the feather motifs.

SALLY BRAMALD   WHEN HEIDE MET SALLY
Quilt dimensions: 58 x 58 in (147 x 147 cm)
Machine foot: Horseshoe-shaped free-motion foot

Sally used a water-soluble rollerball pen to draw the
feather design directly onto this fabulous fabric,
hand-dyed by German dyer Heide Stoll Weber.
Order of machine quilting: The large, central feather
motif is the focus of this quilt. Sally began by
stitching the spine of the feather, one side at a time,
using a lightweight, lilac, fine cotton thread. The idea
was to veil the background with stitched threads to
make the feathers look even brighter.

C. JUNE BARNES SPREAD YOUR WINGS

Quilt dimensions: 87 x 83 in (220 x 210 cm)
Machine foot: No. 9 darning foot

Inspired by a design on a Buddhist priest's mantle,
C. June Barnes marked on the quilt surface the parts
of the design that echo the appliqué designs; the rest
were free-form machine quilted. The appliqué shapes
were quilted and then the inside sections cut away to
reveal an under layer of viscose satin.

Order of machine quilting: The piece is made up of
three panels and was worked in three steps. The first
step was the appliquéd shapes. These were worked
through all layers of the quilt sandwich so that, in
effect, they were quilted once the appliqué process
was completed. The appliquéd shapes were then
echo quilted, also through all layers. The final step
was to outline all the shapes and gradually fill in the
areas in-between.

Decreasing the size of the
motif adds perspective.

Similar motifs are used for
the quilting and the appliqué
to create a sense of unity.

Reverse appliqué, a method that
involves adding fabric layers
beneath the base fabric rather than
above it, adds color and shine to
the quilt.

ELIZABETH BARTON OVERLOOK
Quilt dimensions: 54 x 32 in (137 x 81 cm)
Machine foot: Darning foot with the feed dogs down

The design was based on views of the Smoky Mountains in North Georgia and Western North Carolina in the United States. Elizabeth drives over these mountains in the fall to teach a workshop in Southeast Tennessee, and the colors of the trees and the views from across the hills are what inspired her.

Order of machine quilting: Elizabeth starts her machine quilting by sketching out the design on paper and getting her hand used to the movements necessary to create the design. She uses a rayon thread in a color that enhances the colors in the quilt, usually a slightly deeper tone of the same color as the fabric. Here, she changed the thread color a lot, beginning in the middle and working outward, removing the basting pins gradually. The stitching is applied freehand.

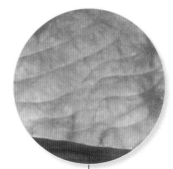

The sky is quilted to suggest the movement of clouds on a windy day.

The quilting emphasizes the fabric pattern.

Rayon thread is used on top and very fine polyster below.

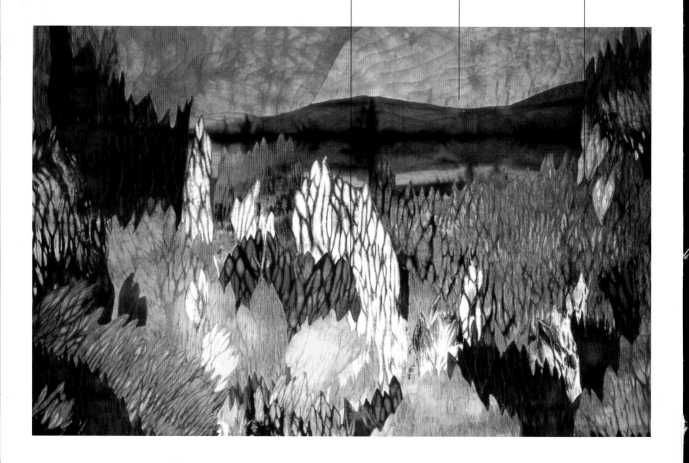

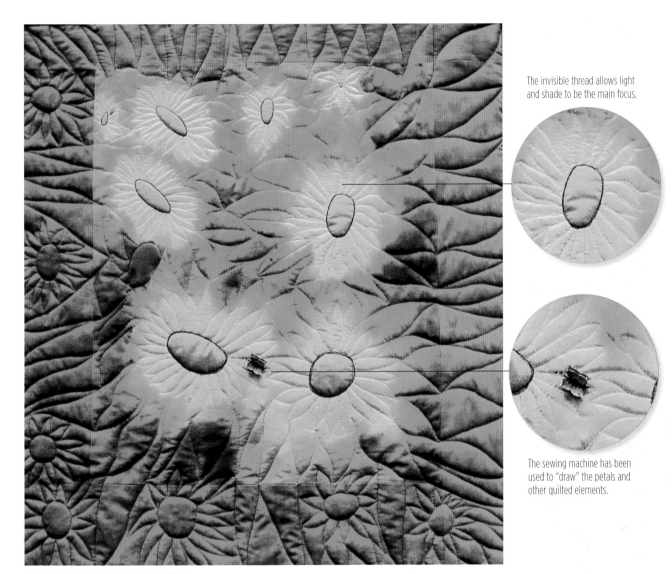

The invisible thread allows light and shade to be the main focus.

The sewing machine has been used to "draw" the petals and other quilted elements.

MARIJKE DE BOER BOON SUNFLOWERS

Quilt dimensions: 30 x 32¹/₂ in (76 x 83 cm)
Machine feet: No. 9 darning foot for Bernina machine 1020

Free-motion quilting was used to "draw" the sunflower and leaf shapes around the tulle flower centers, with the design radiating outward. The quilt top was hand-painted using Procion dyes, and freehand quilted using the dyed areas as a guide.
Order of machine quilting: The quiltmaker began the quilting by anchoring the flower centers and the outer edge of the quilt, then petals were added to form the flowers, and finally leaf shapes filled the border.

ELLIN LARIMER JUNCTIONS III
Quilt dimensions: 43 x 29 in (109 x 73 cm)
Machine foot: Two-sole walking foot
with seam guide

This freehand design is a good
example of the way that Ellin likes to
do her quilting. She pins the backing to
her design wall, then pins the batting
to the backing, then pins the quilt top
to the quilt. She has quilted several
large quilts in sections, then sewn
them together covering the seam with
a strip of the backing.
Order of machine quilting: Ellin's
method is to begin with a color of
thread and generally continue until she
needs to change the thread color. In
this example, she began with the gold.

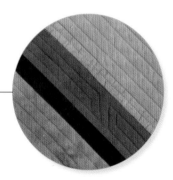

Parallel lines follow the
pieced design.

The quilting is
more subtle on
darker fabrics.

The quilted pattern
spirals outward in an
angular fashion,
adding texture and
movement.

SHEENA J. NORQUAY   100 MARKS
Quilt dimensions: 43 x 43 in (109 x 109 cm)
Machine foot: Darning foot

This decorative wall hanging is an experimental piece using
ten different fillers. The design was rendered freehand without
marking, but the patterns were worked out on paper before
being machine quilted.
Order of machine quilting: Sheena varied the shape, size, and
spacing of each mark as she quilted across the colored strips of
fabric from left to right, using a different color of thread in each
row. On the subject of machine quilting versus hand quilting,
Sheena observes, "it's quicker but not necessarily easier."

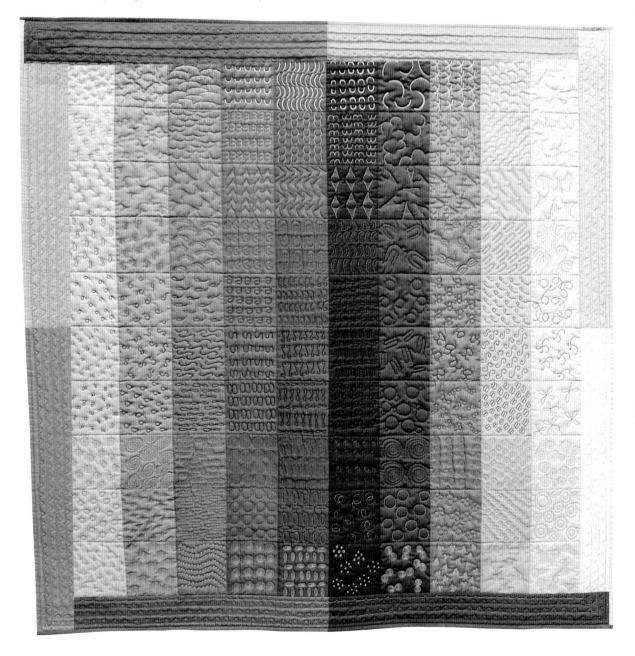

Quilting follows the patchwork seams.

Sweeping parallel lines add movement.

Structured, graphic lines cut across the background between the orange sections.

ELLIN LARIMER   WINGS 2
Quilt dimensions: 31 x 31 in (79 x 79 cm)
Machine foot: Two-sole walking foot
with seam guide

The impetus for the design of this freehand quilt was the desire to break up some of the larger solid areas into smaller sections.
Order of machine quilting: Ellin began with the larger blue and rust colored sections, starting near the middle and quilting out until she arrived at the edge of the quilt.

JERI RIGGS CATS ARE EVERYWHERE
Quilt dimensions: 34 x 48 in (86 x 122 cm)
Machine foot: No. 9 darning foot

This decorative quilt was entirely machine
pieced and appliquéd using batik and
hand-dyed cottons. It was free-motion
quilted with black cotton on the warm-
colored areas and with green rayon thread
on the green background areas.

Order of machine quilting: Jeri used an
all-over flowers-and-leaves theme for
quilting the background freehand.
Beginning at the bottom and working up
to the top of the quilt, she switched to
blue thread to match the sky and quilted
in gentle waves. The warm-colored and
rainbow areas were quilted in black thread
after the background was finished. In
those areas, starting at the center, she
quilted a freehand pattern of flames,
spirals, circles, and blocks, while
incorporating as many cats and birds in
the quilting pattern as seemed to fit
(hence the title). In some areas she cut out
little cats from sticky contact paper and
quilted around them to get the shapes, but
later stitched without marking. Jeri
describes the method as "like doodling
with a sewing machine." The evenness of
the stitching is very important in a quilt
like this—the quilting lines are around ¹/₄ in
(6 mm) apart. Jeri often echos the design
in the fabric itself to get the quilting
pattern, and then elaborates on that idea
in neighboring areas.

A beak, eye, and feathers are implied in
the quilting, which creates character.

The meandering free-
motion quilting includes
many motifs, such as birds.

Cat outlines are incorporated into
the quilted patterns.

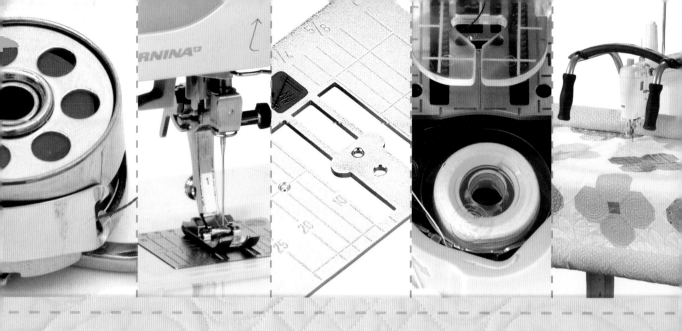

CHAPTER 1
Setting up

In order to enjoy making successful machine-quilted projects, it is imperative that you get to know your machine and become familiar with its functions and attachments. You should also take the time to set out your working environment for optimum comfort.

All about your home sewing machine

All you need to begin machine quilting is a sewing machine with a straight stitch and feed dogs that can be lowered or covered. Wonderful quilts can be completed on good-quality older machines as well as expensive new machines with many added features. Here we look at the components of a modern machine and learn how each each is used in the context of machine quilting.

When learning to use your machine for quilting you will need to become familiar with some functions that you may not have used before. Start by reading up on free-motion quilting—sometimes referred to as "darning"—in the machine's owner's manual. Follow along as the parts and features of the machine are described, and compare them with your machine to familiarize yourself with its capabilities or limitations.

Machine head (1) The head includes the machine bed—the flat surface where the sewing takes place—the machine arm, and the housing that supports the mechanics above the opening. The sewing area is measured from the needle to the side of the opening. The arm length varies from machine to machine, from having about 7 in (18 cm) of space that the quilt bundle must be maneuvered in (regular machine), to having from 9–12 in (23–30 cm) to work within.

Thread spool pin (2) A spool pin (or spindle) holds the spool of thread as the thread is directed through a series of thread guides, between the tension disks, and eventually into the eye of the needle. This machine has a horizontal spool pin that holds a cross-wound spool of thread in place with a thread cap. This same pin can be tilted in an upright position to accommodate a stacked spool of thread. The owner's manual will detail any thread caps, thread retainer disks, and additional spindles that should be used for optimum performance.

Thread path (not shown) The thread path indicates the journey of the thread, beginning at the spool pin and ending in the eye of the needle. The path has a numbered sequence that is often marked in the plastic housing of the machine and printed in the owner's manual. It is important to thread the machine exactly as directed to achieve the tension required for perfectly formed stitches.

Thread guides (3) Thread guides are metal devices that lead the thread to the tension disks or the next guide in the thread path. If any problems occur during sewing, check that the thread is properly inside each guide.

Bobbin winder (4) Most machines have a bobbin winding pin located at the top of the machine, where an empty bobbin is placed for filling, while some have a dedicated motor to wind the bobbin without having to interrupt your sewing—if you unexpectedly run out of bobbin thread. Follow the instructions given in the owner's manual for winding a bobbin properly on your machine. On older or basic models you may need to disengage the fly wheel before winding the bobbin.

Fly wheel (5) The fly wheel (or hand wheel) is located on the right side of the machine. This action is driven by the engine (by pressing the foot control pedal) or by hand. This is an important tool for the machine quilter and is used to adjust precise placement of the needle and to bring the bobbin thread from the back of the quilt up to the top.

Slide-on tray (6) This plastic tray, which comes with the machine, can be used to extend the working area of the machine bed. Some are constructed as a flat tray; some are fashioned into containers that store machine feet and small accessories. The additional work area of the slide-on tray is often large enough for machine quilting small projects.

Stitch length setting (7) The length of the stitches made by your machine may be regulated by a mechanical dial, a sliding lever, or by numbered settings on a computer screen. Stitch length is measured in millimeters or, for older machines, stitches per inch (spi). When free-motion quilting the stitch length setting does not apply because the feed dogs are lowered and do not function to advance the fabric.

10

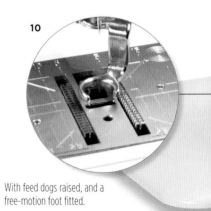

With feed dogs raised, and a free-motion foot fitted.

Stitch width setting (8) The width of the stitch a machine makes can be adjusted for zigzag and decorative stitches. The stitch width is measured from one side to another in millimeters and can vary from 0.5 to 5 mm on most machines, and up to 9 mm on some new machines. If you choose to use a wider stitch for machine quilting, be sure to look at the stitching on the back of the quilt, since some of these stitches were not designed to have the bobbin thread showing.

Stitch plate (9) This is the metal plate beneath the pressure foot. It has open slots for the feed dogs to move within and an opening for the needle. Numbers on the plate give a handy reference guide for seam allowances, measuring the distance from the line to the needle in the center position. A straight stitch machine has a single-hole plate; if you buy a zigzag machine, a zigzag plate comes with it.

Feed dogs (10) These are jagged metal teeth that move up and down to advance the fabric as you sew. The distance they move the fabric is controlled by the stitch length setting. They can be lowered for free-motion quilting by pushing a mechanical button or by choosing the free-motion stitch on some computerized machines.

>> continued over the page

More machine features

Tension disks
These disks adjust the tension of the top thread. A higher number increases the top tension; a lower number decreases it. You need to manually reset the dial for a different weight thread.

Tools settings screen
Computerized machines usually have a screen for tools settings, including adjusting the tension.

Pressure dial
This manual dial adjusts the amount of pressure for the presser foot. You will need to adjust the pressure for different thicknesses of batting.

Feed dogs button
When this button is pressed, the feed dogs are lowered. Press it again to bring the feed dogs back up. On some machines the feed dogs do not pop back up until you begin stitching. Some computerized machines automatically lower the feed dogs when a free-motion function is chosen.

Speed regulation lever/button
This lever raises and lowers the speed that the machine can stitch. For better control, keep it low for intricate designs and when you are learning to quilt.

Bobbin thread cutter
This cuts the bobbin thread, which is particularly helpful when working on a large quilt and access to the underside of the quilt is limited. Different machines leave differing thread-length tails.

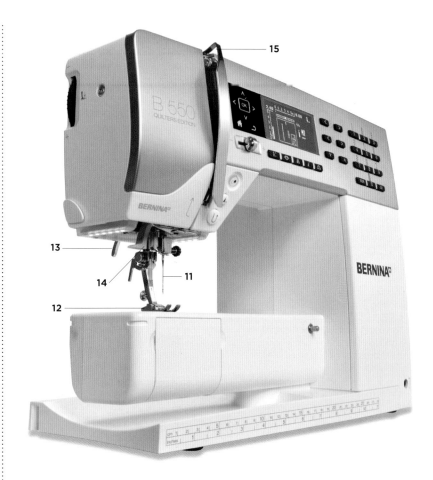

<< continued from previous page

Needles (11) Sewing machine needles are secured in place using the needle screw and screwdriver supplied with with the machine, with the flat side of the needle placed to the back of the machine. Choose the correct size of needle for your thread (see page 67), and one that is manufactured for your type of machine.

Presser foot (12) Various presser feet are available for different tasks.

Presser foot lift lever (13) This lever raises and lowers the presser foot. Some machines have a manual lever operated by hand, and some computerized machines simply lower the foot automatically when the foot pedal is pressed to start sewing. Remember that a manual presser foot lever must be in the raised position when threading the machine, in order to release tension on the tension disks and allow the thread to properly lie between them.

Needle threader (14) Some machines come with a built-in needle threader. It has a very delicate wire loop that enters the needle eye from the back and pulls the top thread through the eye to thread the needle.

Take-up lever (15) This metal lever is a type of thread guide that moves up and down with each rotation of the machine as a stitch is formed. For machine quilting it is important to identify it in its highest position, when the tension of the bobbin thread is released, allowing the bobbin thread to be pulled through to the top.

Top tips for machine maintenance

A well-maintained machine is equally as important as the skill the quilter acquires. Learn how to care for your machine. It is your partner in this work; be good to it and it will serve you well.

• Before you begin a project, clean the machine bed with a slightly damp cloth to remove any dust, dirt, or residue, then buff it dry. Do the same for the extension table or slide-on tray.

• Every time you change the bobbin, clean out the bobbin area with a brush (or a tiny vacuum attachment) to remove lint and any thread ends.

• Clean the feet and feed dogs with a soft brush (a baby's toothbrush makes a wonderful cleaning tool).

• If it is recommended in the owner's manual, oil the upper machine and bobbin, using only the recommended oil. Some machines require a drop of oil in the bobbin race every eight hours. After oiling, stitch on an old cloth to be sure that there is no oil on the thread.

• Begin each project with a fresh needle, and change it again every eight hours. An easy way to keep track of the total time spent stitching is to fill three bobbins—or four if they are small—when you begin the project. When all three—or four—are empty, you have stitched for about eight hours.

BOBBINS

Two threads, one from the spool at the top of the machine and the other from the bobbin, work together to form the machine stitch. The threaded needle passes through the layers of fabric down into the hole of the stitch plate. As it completes its journey to the lowest position and begins to move back up, a loop of top thread is formed. At that moment the bobbin shuttle rotates and the hook grabs the top loop and wraps it around the bobbin case, catching the bobbin thread. When the needle returns to its highest position, the threads should lock with one another in the middle of the fabric layers.

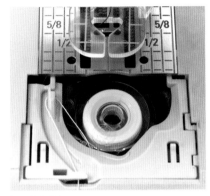

Drop-in bobbin
This machine has a drop-in bobbin. The bobbin nestles in laying flat. Follow the instructions given in the owner's manual to thread the bobbin case correctly.

Set-in bobbin
This machine uses a bobbin case to hold the bobbin. A door in the front of the machine arm opens to reveal the place to insert the bobbin case.

ADJUSTING BOBBIN TENSION

Some bobbin cases have a metal screw that adjusts the tension of the different weight threads. Test for correct tension by placing the filled bobbin in the case, with the thread through the tension slot; then hold the bobbin case in your hand and tug on the thread. If the case lifts and then slowly slides back into your hand, the tension is ideal. If the bobbin spins in the case, the tension is too loose. If the case won't slide down, the tension is too tight. When making adjustments to the screw for different weight threads, begin by making a note of where the factory set tension is before you adjust it. Look at the screw as a dial on a clock and turn it in tiny, one-hour increments.

Pin pointers
Some quilters prefer to purchase a separate bobbin case and use it only for lightweight threads without changing the factory setting on the original case. Paint a dot of nail polish on the case to distinguish the adjusted bobbin from the original.

By purchasing extra bobbins and filling several before you begin sewing, you can save time and avoid the annoyance of having to stop mid-flow to fill a bobbin.

Some bobbin cases have a hole in the finger that is threaded for extra bobbin tension. This is useful when you don't want to see any bobbin thread on the top.

Other machines

As discussed previously, you can complete all your machine quilting projects using a home sewing machine. However, you may have come across some of the other machines available to the modern quilter, each with their own advantages and disadvantages.

LONGARM QUILTING MACHINE

Longarm quilting machines consist of a large machine head, mounted on a racking system, that moves from side to side on a long table. Originally designed for commercial use, and for making large bedspreads, these dedicated straight stitch machines were suitable for fast stitching using durable thread, large needles, and a bobbin rotation calibrated for large stitches. Current machines can handle the lightweight threads and finer needles needed to form tiny stitches for refined free-motion quilting, and built-in stitch regulators have improved the resulting stitch quality. A longarm system takes up a lot of space and money, with prices starting at US$10,000 and stretching to over US$35,000.

With this system it is not necessary to baste the quilt layers, rather each layer is held taut on a separate roller that is supported by the table. Computerized operating systems can be programmed to calculate the number of motifs needed to fill a space so that the operator can walk away and let the machine stitch automatically.

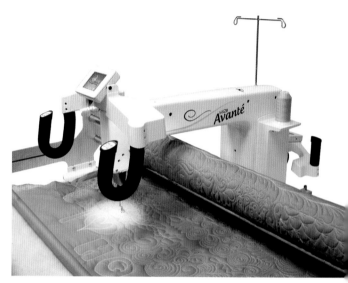

This longarm machine can be operated from the front or back.

MIDARM MACHINE

A midarm quilting system offers a midsize (larger than domestic; smaller than longarm) industrial machine head, mounted on a large table. These dedicated straight stitch quilting machines give the quilter plenty of space to maneuver the quilt bundle. Like a domestic machine, the machine head stays stationary and the quilt bundle is moved by the seated operator. Stitching can be performed anywhere on the quilt. Since the machine head sits on a large table and there is no roller system, pin basting the quilt bundle is necessary.

As with the longarm, this machine was developed for commercial work, but can be adapted for refined stitching.

DOMESTIC MACHINE WITH A FRAME

This system uses a regular size or stretch model domestic sewing machine mounted on a rack, with the individual layers of the quilt attached to rollers. Handles attached to the machine allow you to move it back and forth across a narrow strip of exposed quilt. The operator stands or uses a rolling chair. One advantage to this system is that, because the quilt layers are attached to rollers, basting is not necessary. However, it can take some time to accurately load the layers on the rollers so that they are not misaligned. The rollers can also cause space issues, since the take-up roller that holds the completed section of the quilt is between the needle and head opening and, unless you are using a stretch model, that space can be quite narrow. As the top is quilted the space gets smaller as the rolled-up quilt fills the machine throat, sometimes limiting access to the stitching area to 4 in (10 cm). Planning designs to fit that narrow space, or interlock with one another, may be tricky and time consuming.

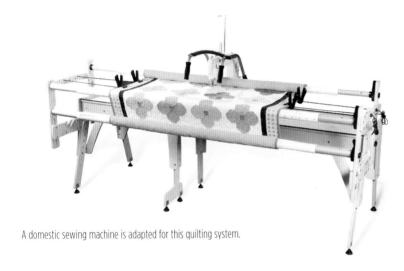

A domestic sewing machine is adapted for this quilting system.

DOMESTIC MACHINE WITHOUT A FRAME

A stretch model like this offers you more space to maneuver the quilt bundle. You can plan quilting designs that flow anywhere on the quilt surface because you have the freedom to access the entire quilt. These machines require little or no adjustments when using fine thread. There are no rollers to hold the layers so they must be basted. Always position a stretch model on a large work surface.

Personal note from the author

The key to using a domestic machine for quilting is how the quilt bundle is maneuvered under the needle and how choosing the right supplies makes that job much simpler. I am delighted with the results I can accomplish with my domestic machines and have no desire to change. For me, at this moment, the investment in a longarm would be an expense I could not justify. My aspirations have never been geared toward making quilts to sell or to transform someone else's top into a quilt. I love to draw, write, teach, and create designs for you. So here are the reasons I continue to use a regular-size domestic machine for quilting:

• **Space, or lack of it:** I simply do not want to dedicate space in my home for a longarm machine.
• **Practicality:** I already own several domestic machines.
• **Unrestricted design possibilities:** Having access to the entire surface does not limit the quilting potential. Plus, many designs I create require maneuvering intricate motifs; my machine was built to handle it.
• **Delicacy of the results:** My stitches are tiny and the thread is lightweight.
• **Logistics:** I teach on domestic machines so that students can learn on their own equipment in class.

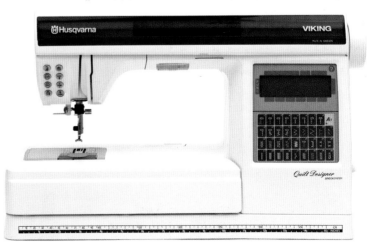

With a stretch model you have more room to move your bundle as you sew.

Attachments and accessories

Machine quilting does not require a fancy, computerized sewing machine or extensive attachments. Having said that, there are some wonderful new advancements and notions available to make your machine quilting go more smoothly. Some of the accessories described here are included with selected models; some will have to be purchased separately.

If you haven't visited your sewing machine dealer in a while, go in to see what new attachments they offer. Tell them what you want to do with the machine, and have them show you how they would use the accessories. Don't be afraid to try something new; it is only a bit of fabric and a few hours of your time. Here are some must-haves and luxury items for the beginner and advanced machine quilter.

Knee lift bar (1) This metal rod fits into a hole in the front of the machine and extends down to your knee. By pressing the bar with your knee you can raise and lower the presser foot without removing your hands from the work. Many machine quilters find the knee lift bar invaluable when maneuvering the quilt.

Walking foot (2) For straight stitching quilt bundles a walking foot is attached to the machine to replace the presser foot. It works to advance the three individual layers of the quilt bundle from the top in conjunction with the feed dogs, which move the fabric from the bottom. Without a walking foot, the layers will shift, causing puckering.

Stitch regulator (3) When the feed dogs are lowered for free-motion quilting, the machine's stitch length setting disengages, which is when stitch regulators may come in handy. A laser scans how far the fabric is moved and tells the machine to take another stitch, thus ensuring that the length of the stitches is consistent. Try one out before you purchase, making sure it does not block your view and prevent you from seeing where you need to guide the needle.

Extension table (4) An extension table should be purchased for a specific model—to extend the work surface at the height of the machine bed.

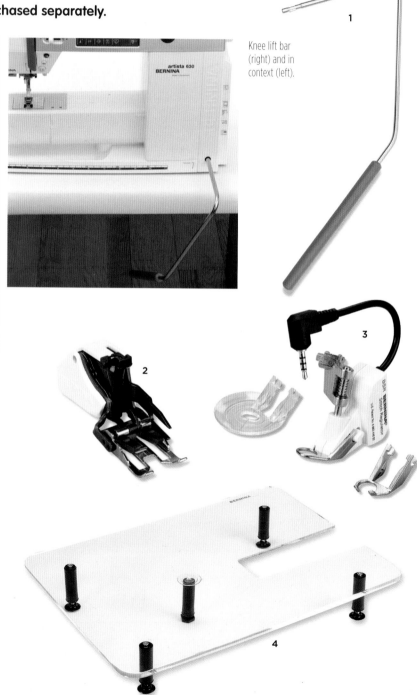

Knee lift bar (right) and in context (left).

Single-hole stitch plate (5) A single-hole stitch plate keeps the surface completely level, preventing the layers from being pushed down into a wider opening. This special stitch plate is sold as an attachment, and assists the machine in making perfectly straight stitches. It is also great for piecing triangular patchwork.

Free-motion foot (6) The free-motion foot, used with the feed-dogs lowered, allows lines of stitching to occur in any direction the quilt is moved. It is important to have the appropriate foot for each machine quilting task, a broad foot for large utilitarian stitches and a small, open-toe style (shown right) for refined work. For more on free-motion quilting, turn to page 80.

Safety pins (7) Quilts are basted with safety pins, which are available in several sizes. Inexpensive, tiny gold safety pins ($^3/_4$–1 in [2–2.5 cm] long) are lightweight and leave a small hole in the fabric.

Snips (8) These sharp fabric scissors with a curved blade enable you to clip threads right against the surface of the quilt.

Tweezers (9) Tweezers are useful for picking up anything that is too tiny to grab with your fingers. Use them to grasp the bobbin thread when bringing it up at the beginning of stitching, or to eliminate loose threads or lint from the stitching area. A loop of masking tape also works well.

Seam ripper (10) A very fine and sharp seam ripper is useful if you want to remove unwanted stitches.

Self-healing cutting mat, rotary cutter, and clear plastic rulers (11) These tools make up a time-effective cutting system for greater accuracy when cutting fabric.

Masking tape is good for basting. Keep a loop of it handy to pick up loose threads.

Spray starch is used to stabilize fabric to avoid stretching during cutting, piecing, marking, and quilting. You can use commercial spray starch or mix your own from liquid starch—sold in grocery stores—or by following the mixing directions on a box of dry cornstarch.

Lint brush rids the bobbin area of lint.

Machine oil can be useful for sewing machine lubrication. Only use oil recommended for your machine.

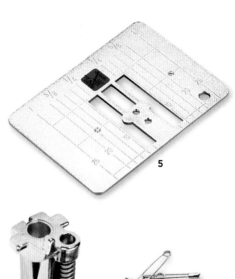

5

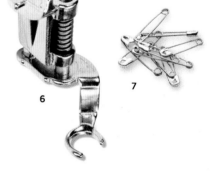

6

7

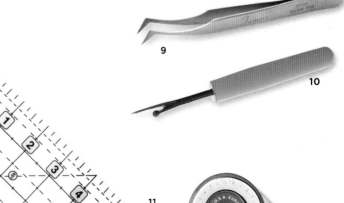

8

9

10

11

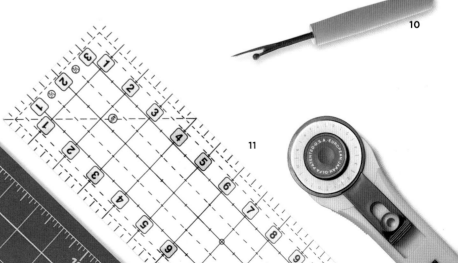

Setting up your work space

Whether your project is large or small, setting up your work space properly will enhance your quilting experience and avoid stress on your body.

Quilter's dream work space
You may not have the space for an arrangement like this, but you might like to apply some of these tips to your existing work space.

Floor-standing magnifying lamp creates optimal conditions for intricate quilting.

Portable toolbox contains everything you need for the project at hand.

Pin up a fabric you like or test out color combinations and layout on a design wall.

Add this book to your quilting library.

A north-facing window guarantees even light.

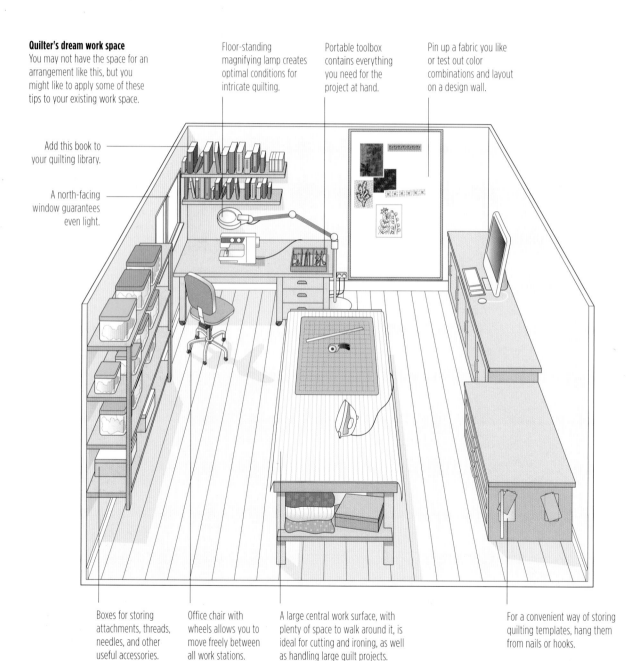

Boxes for storing attachments, threads, needles, and other useful accessories.

Office chair with wheels allows you to move freely between all work stations.

A large central work surface, with plenty of space to walk around it, is ideal for cutting and ironing, as well as handling large quilt projects.

For a convenient way of storing quilting templates, hang them from nails or hooks.

FINDING A WORK SURFACE

Being comfortable will make you want to be at your machine longer, and being at your machine longer will get your projects completed sooner. Providing proper support for the entire quilt sandwich is key to keeping it under control when machine quilting. To achieve a consistent stitch length, the work area must be large enough to support the weight of the quilt, so it doesn't hang off the edges and pull the thread, which would distort the stitches. A table height of about 30 in (76 cm) should allow your elbows to bend at a 90-degree angle. Placing the table or sewing cabinet up against a wall or in a corner prevents the quilt from falling over the edge. You can also add a rolling thread drawer or ironing board (placed to the left of your chair) to support the quilt.

QUILT SIZE CONSIDERATIONS

Consider whether you will work with your machine in a cabinet specifically designed to hold it, or place it on a work table. Quilting a small piece is a simple job compared to dealing with a large quilt. You can easily slip it out from under the needle any time you want to check the stitching on the back or snip the threads. The machine's slide-on tray may be a large enough work area for a small project, and it allows your elbows to relax. When working on a large piece the size of the person doing the quilting, as well as the size of the quilt, can determine what strategy works best, since the height of the quilter may impact on the way that they handle a large bundle. When the machine is mounted close to the front edge of the cabinet there is nowhere for a large quilt to go but over the shoulder or in the lap. Some quilters roll a large quilt, working with the roll over their shoulder while they stitch. If you want to work this way, wear a slippery shirt so that the quilt does not stick to your clothing.

Another method involves setting the machine on a large table for part, or all, of the machine quilting process. Place it 10–12 in (25–30 cm) in from the front edge, with enough space on the right side for easy access to small tools. This allows space for the quilt to rest on the table in front of you, with your elbows extended in a relaxed, slightly downward bend. Try this method during the anchoring process, when you need your large motor skills to maneuver the entire quilt. You can always put the machine back in the cabinet after you have anchored the quilt into work zones for a closer focus of the refined areas.

SEATING AND POSTURE

Use an office chair with good back support and adjustable height. Sit at the machine with the center of your body aligned with the needle of the machine, without twisting the spine. Sit squarely on the chair, not on the edge of your seat. When your body is not in its most relaxed position, it will show up in your quilting. Adjust the height of your chair to avoid straining your neck. There will be times when you need to sit higher to see the work, and others when you want to focus in on smaller details and lower the chair a bit—however, not so low that your elbows are held up at an uncomfortable position. If your chair is not adjustable, you can add a chair pad for extra height when necessary.

Correct sitting position
Avoid stress on your lower back and arms by sitting with your chair placed close enough to the machine to avoid leaning toward the quilt when you work. Sit squarely on the chair, with your body on the center of the seat to have the best control of the bundle.

Incorrect sitting position
Avoid sitting on the edge of your chair, with your arms stretched out. You will have less control in this awkward position.

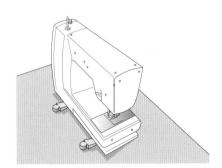

Use door stops
Position two door stops (purchased at a hardware store) under the back of the machine to tilt it forward so that the arm of the machine does not block your view of the work area.

Magnifier attachment
This magnifying lens was manufactured to be attached to a specific machine. It works well to enlarge the work area around the needle.

LIGHTING AND MAGNIFICATION

Staring at close-up work for long periods of time can tire your eyes, and the built-in light on some machines, especially older models, may not be adequate. Quilting with dark colors or doing refined work is especially straining for the eyes, as is working with thread that matches the fabric, so you might consider using additional lighting, and possibly magnification.

Some machines have a "U" shaped light on three sides above the needle, and a long tube of light along the underside of the arm. Others have a natural spectrum bulb that can be adjusted to the color of the thread for the best view of intricate work.

Machine manufacturers also offer a magnifier attachment that can be screwed onto the machine just above the needle. It magnifies the area well, but needs to be removed to access the needle.

You can position an additional lamp or work light on the table to the left of the machine, close to the needle. This works fine for a small project, but gets in the way of larger projects. A swing-arm light that attaches to the table with a clamp will provide needed light but may add unwanted heat, or vibrate when the machine is running.

A magnifying lamp—with extra light and magnification all in one—could be the perfect solution. Magnifying lamps are available as floor-standing models or with a clamp-style assembly that can be attached to your table. The light is placed in front of you, between your face and the work. Not only does the bulb stay relatively cool, but you won't feel any heat that it is does generate because it is in front of you. Nor will your body movements cause a shadow on the work. This style of light is available in different quality and price ranges. The lower quality ones can be found in large sewing centers and craft stores, the best ones are of a very high quality and are sold in needlework shops, medical supply stores, and stores for the visually impaired.

Magnifying lamp
A magnifying lamp provides supplementary light and magnification in one.

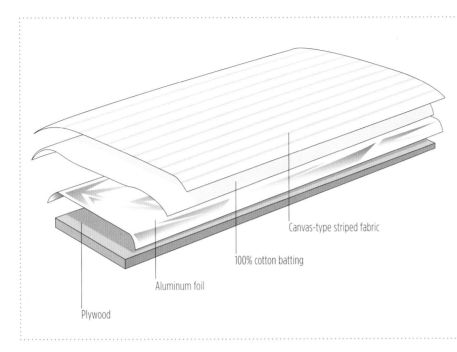

Canvas-type striped fabric

100% cotton batting

Aluminum foil

Plywood

Make your own large ironing board

1 Cut a board to fit your support system from a solid wooden board or plywood (avoid chipboard that may disintegrate from heat).
2 Purchase a top fabric with vertical stripes to use as alignment guides.
3 Assemble the ironing board by stapling these layers to the back of the plywood.
• First, a layer of aluminum foil, shiny side up to reflect the heat.
• Next, a thin layer of 100% cotton or Insul-brite® heat-resistant batting, which will protect the surface and reflect the heat back into the fabric.
• Finally, a layer of heavy, canvas-type fabric of 100% cotton.

IRONING SURFACES

To achieve fine results when machine quilting, you must begin with a top that is accurately cut and pieced. Pressing each seam open is a good way of evenly distributing the layers of fabric to avoid mountains of seams that interrupt your stitching rhythm and stitch length consistency.

A large, conveniently placed pressing surface is a valuable component of the sewing space set-up. However, if you do not have a dedicated sewing room and are limited on space, your work area may not allow for such luxury. Consider placing a large, padded board on top of your cutting surface or on top of some storage shelving. Make it as large as your space allows, overhanging the top of the shelving to gain added surface. The larger the surface, the better it will accommodate the quilt top, and the better it will be for pressing bolt fabric before it is cut. When not in use, you can slide it behind a piece of furniture for storage. For sharp and accurate pressing, the surface should be firm, not a spongy foam pad that allows the iron to sink in, so use batting covered with a cotton canvas-type striped fabric, as suggested above.

You may also want to keep a smaller pressing pad handy—convenient for a quick press close enough to the stitching, and you won't have to get up from the machine when you are assembling patchwork.

PURCHASING AN IRON

A good, hot iron is an essential tool for producing neat and accurate patchwork, and for stabilizing fabric that will not stretch when cutting, marking, basting, and quilting. With manufacturers attempting to avoid liability due to injury, it has become a difficult task to find a good iron. Here are some suggestions:

• Black and Decker seem to make the hottest irons. Their travel-size iron is hot and has a long cord.
• Purchase an old iron from an estate sale or church rummage sale. You may be lucky enough to find one with a smooth metal plate without any steam holes.
• Steam is not necessary and can actually stretch fabrics.

A good-quality iron is essential for any machine quilter, beginner or advanced.

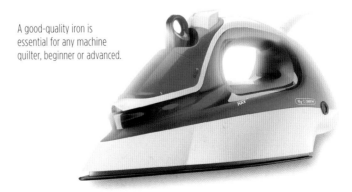

CHAPTER 2
Before you quilt

Using your home sewing machine to quilt requires different preparations for assembling the quilt top, marking, or basting the layers than those used when hand quilting or sending a top out to a longarm quilter. In this chapter you will learn which fabrics, batting, and thread are appropriate for each project, and how to prepare the fabric for cutting, marking, and basting.

What is a quilt top?

A quilt top might be pieced together from a number of patchwork or appliqué blocks, or take the form of a solid fabric with a quilting design stitched over it. The possibilities for the layout of the quilt top are endless; it is rare to see two alike.

PATCHWORK

Patchwork refers to the process of cutting up the fabric into little pieces and then sewing it back together into a larger piece. The following terms are commonly used when discussing a patchwork quilt:

- **Patches** are the small squares or triangles that are sewn together into rows that make a block.
- **Blocks** are the squares, strips, and triangles sewn into rows creating many different patchwork patterns.
- **Setting and corner triangles** are used to fill the spaces at the end of the rows and in the corners when the blocks are set on point (with their corners pointing up and down).
- **Rows** are the blocks (and sashings if used) joined into strips.
- **The quilt center** is constructed from the assembled rows.
- **Borders** are the strips of fabric that can be added to the quilt center. A quilt may have one, several, or no borders. Borders may also be rows of small assembled patches.

This patchwork by JOANIE ZEIER POOLE features nine basket blocks with sashing strips set on point in the center of the layout. Corner triangles of fabric provide a space for impressive motifs. Various borders, including a sawtooth patchwork border, frame the center panel.

Anatomy of a quilt bundle

Quilt top The outer layer of the quilt that is seen when the quilt is displayed on a bed, table, or wall. This may take the form of assembled patchwork or appliqué blocks, or a solid fabric designed to show quilted motifs and textures only.

Batting The center layer of the quilt. There are many batting materials to choose from, and in varying thicknesses. See pages 58–59 to learn more.

Backing The bottom layer of the quilt that keeps the batting inside. See pages 52–53 for advice on choosing suitable fabrics.

Quilt top

Batting

Backing

The bird body and wing shapes have their edges turned under and were appliquéd by hand.

Mock hand appliqué by machine was used to appliqué these shapes with a $\frac{1}{8}$-in (3-mm) seam allowance turned to the back.

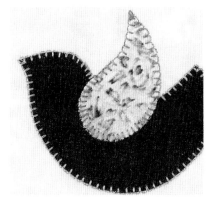

The bird body and wing shapes had a paper-backed fusible web applied to the back of the fabric; then the shapes were drawn on the paper and cut out before being permanently fused to the base fabric.

Paper-backed fusible web was applied to the back of the printed fabric then the bird and flowers were cut out and arranged on the base fabric and permanently fused in place.

WHOLECLOTH

A wholecloth quilt top consists of a solid fabric (this may be pieced to attain the preferred size) which is quilted with decorative designs following lines that have been marked on the fabric.

APPLIQUÉ

Appliqué is the art of attaching shapes cut out of fabric to a base fabric. This versatile technique can include:

- **Turned edge by hand** The appliqué shape is cut larger than the finished size and the edges are turned under by hand and held to the base with hand stitching.
- **Turned edge by machine** The appliqué shape is cut larger than the finished size and the edges are turned under and held to the base with machine stitches.
- **Raw-edge fusible appliqué** The shapes are held to the base using a layer of fusible web that attaches them permanently. The edge of the appliqué shape is not turned under.
- **Broderie perse** Appliqué shapes are cut from a printed fabric and applied in a specific arrangement with fusible web—or are stitched to the base by hand or machine.

This wholecloth quilt by JOANIE ZEIER POOLE uses a simple, elegant motif in a variety of different combinations to fill the quilt top. A formal grid anchors the flourished border pattern.

Purpose and planning

It is so much fun to plan a new project. Spend some time thinking about how the quilt will be used to best determine the supplies you need and the construction techniques you will use.

Order of work

1 Measure the wall, table, or bed and calculate the quilt dimensions.

2 Draft a finished size layout, including the details for piecing, appliqué, and borders.

3 Indicate the color, pattern scale, and value of the fabric selections, placed to best accentuate any patchwork or appliqué.

4 Collect quilting designs.

5 Calculate the yardage needed and purchase the fabric. Select the thread and needles based on the look and durability required.

6 Purchase batting based on durability and performance.

7 For patchwork, assemble a practice block and determine a pressing plan for each seam.

8 Assemble the pieced top.

9 Do a final pressing of the top.

10 Mark the quilting designs on the top.

11 Assemble and stabilize the backing fabric.

12 Pin-baste the layers into a quilt bundle.

WHAT IS THE PURPOSE OF THE QUILT?

The reason you make a quilt will vary with each project. Consider the durability required, which dictates the supply choices, and the scale and intricacy of the quilting designs. When making a quilt to cover a person, on the sofa or in bed, the batting should be drapable and able to keep them warm in the winter and cool in the summer. For an heirloom or treasured keepsake your plan may include elaborate patchwork, appliqué, or wholecloth layout. The quilting designs could incorporate dates, names, and images relevant to the recipient or to the occasion for which the quilt is made, requiring many hours of detailed work. Supplies chosen for a rarely used piece could include specialty fabrics and elegant silk thread. Or, is this quilt for a baby's crib? Choose easy-care fabric and durable thread that will hold up to frequent washings, and a natural fiber batting that will not trap moisture against the baby's skin.

WHAT AM I CAPABLE OF MAKING?

Another matter to consider is the construction process. Realistically, what are your assembly and quilting abilities? If you are a beginner and your patchwork skills are not perfected, your only machine quilting option may be to meander all over the quilt top (see Stippling, pages 82–83). As your skills in piecing increase you can plan to stitch in the ditch—on the seam lines—or use geometrically accurate quilting.

What about a deadline? Some quilters plan an extravagant project intended as a gift for a special occasion, and fail to be realistic about the time it will take. The size, the number of blocks to assemble or appliqué, and the more quilting you plan, the longer it will take to complete. If the baby is due in four weeks it may be a good idea to forget the entire nursery ensemble and consider an adorable bib project that can be stitched in an afternoon (see page 110).

Calculating measurements

You will need to accurately measure the space that the quilt will occupy and transfer the measurement to graph paper.

Bed quilt
Measure the top of the mattress and draw it on the graph paper. Add the length of the drop on the two sides and foot (to the floor for a bedspread or just below the mattress for a comforter). Plan the layout so no patchwork block is halfway on the top and halfway hanging off the side. Consider if the head end of the quilt will be covered by pillows or if it will cover the pillows. If it covers pillows, measure them, add for the tuck, and draw that on the plan. If the project is for a split king, consider making two twin size coverlets that are easier to maneuver during the quilting process, easier to store, and not so heavy to sleep under.

Wall quilt
When planning a wall quilt, measure the space where the quilt will hang and draw it on the graph paper. Be sure to plan the final border fabric to contrast with the wall color.

Table runner
Consider whether a table runner should fit the center of the table or flow off the ends and, if so, by how much. Be sure to accommodate for the size of the plates. Measure the length of the table, add the drop if desired, and draw the outline on the graph paper.

DRAWING A LAYOUT ON GRAPH PAPER

By creating a precise plan thorough to the last detail, you can calculate the amount of fabric to buy, the number of blocks to make, and the size of the quilting designs needed.

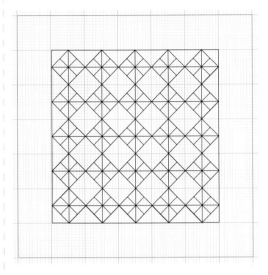

1 After measuring the space that the finished quilt will occupy, draw the outline on graph paper with one square on the paper representing 1 in (2.5 cm) of the quilt. Draw the quilt center with the patchwork or appliqué blocks. Here we used five rows of five pinwheel blocks set on point with solid blocks between them. Indicate the setting triangles and corner triangles.

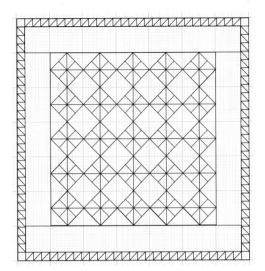

2 Add the borders that fill the space out to the outline. The sawtooth border complements the geometric pattern of the central patchwork layout in this example.

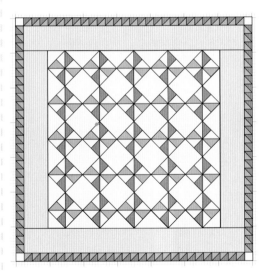

3 Color the spaces to represent the fabric choices. Here we went for a simple pink and yellow color scheme.

4 Overlay the quilting designs in open spaces and over patchwork blocks where intended.

Choosing a quilting design

Quilting is all about the stitching that holds the three layers of material together. The designs you choose to stitch add embellishment, movement, excitement, and texture, so it's important to consider what you might use and where.

When you plan the quilting for a project, think about how much time you wish to devote to the process. Just how difficult is the design choice compared to your skill level? If you begin your project with unrealistic expectations of your time commitment or your abilities, you may add unnecessary stress to the situation. Edge-to-edge meandering may only take a weekend for a queen size quilt; however, the same piece may take several months for tiny heirloom work. On the other hand, a beautiful, intricate quilting design can get you really interested in machine quilting.

The important thing to think about when planning for machine quilting is that you need to be able to stitch with continuous lines of thread, and have as few starts and stops as possible. This can be accomplished by avoiding isolated motifs, placing quilting motifs on outlines of spaces, and connecting the motifs into rows and groups with the outlines touching.

When you are adding the quilting designs to your plan, keep in mind that all of the quilting, both motifs and fillers, needs to be evenly distributed throughout the entire quilt. If some areas feature heavily quilted designs saturated with stitching, while others have little or no stitching, the quilt be distorted and have wavy edges, and the areas left without quilting will look unfinished.

FINDING AND USING MOTIFS

When looking for designs to enhance the theme of your quilt, the quilting world itself offers an extensive range of patterns. Over the next few pages we look at options for sourcing and using designs. Photocopy and play with design choices to see how they might fill your layout. If they do not fit the spaces, adjust the size of the designs accordingly.

Free-motion quilting makes it easy to add interest to your plan with decorative motifs and background fillers. Start with simple motifs that are easy to stitch. Repeating the same motif in the various areas of the layout is an element of good design, while stitching the same shape again and again is also a great skill-building exercise.

Quilting stencils
Plastic stencils are available in many traditional designs. They can easily be traced with water-soluble markers and pencils.

Design choices

Options for simple effort
- Create straight lines using a walking foot.
- Simple free-motion designs.

Options for adding a customized, personalized pizzazz
- Free-motion stitch designs that fit the large open areas and borders.
- Coordinate designs for multi-size borders, blocks, and setting triangles.

Options for heirloom commitment
- Choose a theme, and then coordinate fabric, pattern, and quilting designs.
- Customize images, lettering, and dates.
- Include background fillers.

Quilting books
Quilting books or printed designs (like those at the back of this book), offer a wide array of patterns to keep you stitching for a lifetime.

Presented on this page is a collection of quilting designs originating from the elegant Quinn quilting motif by Joanie Zeier Poole. Many variations are achieved by manipulating all or parts of this motif, inspired by the timeless fleur-de-lis.

FOCUS DESIGNS

Take the guesswork out of planning wonderful quilts by using one simple motif and its many variations. You can create squares, corner and setting triangles, and wide and narrow borders, each utilizing common elements that complement one another. Make several copies of the design to test for size and positioning—for example, one flipped up and one down, as pairs, or on their sides—to add variety to the layout.

1+2 Block designs: four Quinn motifs are joined in the center of these blocks with a double outline of a circle. Two variations are created simply by orienting the motif to the top of the block or toward the corners.
3 Setting triangle: to fill the larger setting triangular space along the sides of a layout with patchwork or appliqué blocks are set on point.
4 Corner triangle: this motif is used to fill a corner space when a patchwork or appliqué quilt has blocks set on point.

5 Motifs used as a pair: the motif is reflected with the base of one motif touching the base of another, and can be used in rows to fill wide border spaces.
6 Wreath design: six motifs resting on a circle can be used to fill large, plain blocks or the center of a wholecloth quilt.

BORDER DESIGNS

Borders, whether narrow or wide, can be filled with combinations of motifs. Use these examples as inspiration and try some variations with your own motifs. Since each plan has the motifs resting on an outline of the space to be filled, that line is used as a road when stitching to the next motif.

1 A narrow border is filled with the Quinn motif directed toward the outside of the quilt. A very simple variation of overlapping motifs forms a graceful arch connecting the motifs in the corner.

2 In this narrow border design, Quinn motifs point toward the quilt center and a portion of a motif evenly distributes the quilting in the corner.

3 When the Quinn motif is reflected at the base, and displayed in a row, an elegant circular subdesign is formed. Here, sections of the overlapping motifs were blended and removed to form a pleasing corner.

4 The Quinn block design was divided with half resting on each border outline. Notice how portions of the motif are placed on the diagonal to fill the empty corner space.

1

2

3

4

BACKGROUND FILLERS

Background fillers include numerous patterns that fill the quilt surface with wonderful texture. The time to decide if background fillers will be used for a quilt is when you are creating your layout. You may want to quickly complete a project by simply filling the entire top with a grid or meandering. Or you may wish to use tiny background fillers to flatten the background around motifs. If that is the case, be sure the motifs are large enough to contrast with the scale of the filler.

The patterns can be divided into two groups, free-form fillers, where the stitching is simply directed by a pattern imprinted on your brain, and formal fillers, which are based on a marked line, circle, or grid, a foundation that is followed to create a pattern.

You can include free-form background fillers on your plan, but they will not be marked on the quilt top; rather these patterns are stitched from ideas in the mind of the quilter. They are more random, not necessarily perfectly repeated forms (see page 87). Formal fillers may require marking of circles, curved or straight lines, or grids (see page 88). These lines may be followed with stitching to create numerous patterns including checkerboards, basket weaves, and square or diamond-shaped crossed lines.

1 Grid on point is a formal filler that is marked on the quilt top and is stitched after the motif has been stitched.

2 The channel quilted background filler is a formal filler that is marked on the quilt and filled in after the motif has been stitched.

3 A small, free-form pebble filler surrounds and fills the area around the motif. The scale of this filler will ensure that the pebble design will not overwhelm the motif but create a balanced and even texture.

4 The area where the echo line that surrounds an outline meets the lines echoing another outline offers an opportunity for interesting sub-patterns to form. It is always a good idea to practice stitching this filler, because the last few rounds can produce some awkward spaces and the drawn line is different from the stitches.

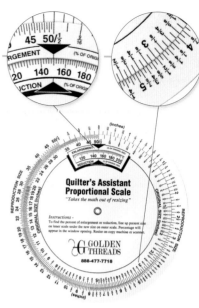

RESIZING DESIGNS

Sometimes the design or block needs to be made larger or smaller to fit your layout. A proportion scale can be purchased at a quilt shop or from your office supply store. Or you could ask to borrow one at a copy center—they will have one available for you to use.

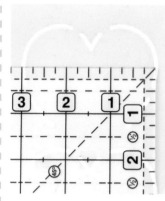

1 Measure the stencil: this is the original size.

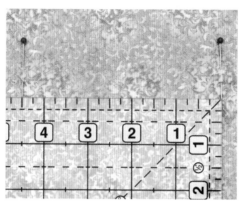

2 Measure the space you need to fill: this is the reproduction size.

3 Rotate the wheel to align both measurements. Look in the box for the percentage of enlargement or reduction to set the copy machine to.

MAKING MULTIPLE COPIES OF THE SAME DESIGN

For multiple copies of the same design, pierce stacks of Golden Threads quilting paper.

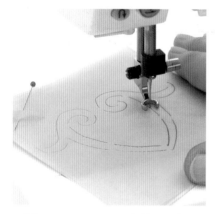

1 Cut as many squares as needed from quilting paper, the size of the block. Pin or staple the stack together. Draw the design on the top layer. Pierce through the stack over the design lines using a sewing machine without thread (alternatively, use a large needle).

2 Pin the pierced paper squares in position on the layered quilt top.

3 Now simply stitch through the paper designs. Remove all paper gently, without tugging on the stitches.

Making and using templates

Here is a technique for planning the quilting designs from your graph paper plan or for a quilt top that is already assembled. Simply measure the block or border space that you want to design for, and use any craft paper (or clear plastic sheets) to make full-size templates to determine perfectly fitting designs. Copy several motifs, flip and rotate them to fill the space, and use the template when tracing the design on the quilt.

Setting triangle with a paper template.

For pieced blocks, audition several design choices by tracing them on a piece of tracing paper or a sheet of clear plastic transparency. Play with full motifs or just parts of a motif. Try dividing the block in quarters, on the straight and on the diagonal. Observe the different looks you can get by placing a motif on each line or in each section of the divide.

For a setting triangle, make a paper template the finished size of the triangle and play with placement of full or partial motifs to evenly fill the space.

Patchwork blocks with acetate overlay...

...auditioned in two different ways.

PAPER TEMPLATES FOR BORDERS

Cut a paper template the width and length of the longest edge of the border and, if you intend to miter the corners, fold the ends at a 45-degree angle. Fold the paper in half horizontally and draw a line lengthwise down the center as a guide for accurate placement. Begin with the motifs in the center working toward the corner or start in the corner and work toward the center. If the motifs do not meet, add a partial motif or a small design like a circle or heart, or just leave space to fill with a background filler.

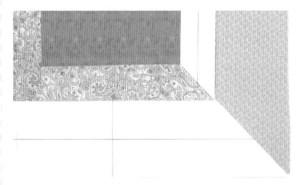

Templates are needed for each size of border used in the quilt.

A pair of motifs are placed on the center fold and aligned with the center line of the template.

Planning for a patchwork quilt

There are no rules for stitching the layers of a patchwork quilt together, but there are helpful guidelines to follow that will make the job simpler.

Patchwork tops can be quilted with straight lines or curved patterns. Stitching can be formal or informal depending on your choices. A bit of extra thought when you are assembling the top will provide you with the most options for machine quilting.

Your plan for quilting a patchwork top will be different for each top you make. If you have sewn many small colorful pieces into patterns or blocks, you may decide that the patchwork is the star of the piece and use stitch in the ditch—stitching on the existing seam lines—to hold the layers together. However, a closer examination of the construction of the top may determine that is not the best choice. Depending on the accuracy of your assembly, ditch quilting may not be possible. Imagine trying to follow a seam line that jumps even an eighth of an inch at every intersection. In that case, you could choose to free-motion quilt an all-over pattern or large meandering to avoid bulky intersections.

Construct a practice block to plan how to press each seam before you assemble the necessary stack of blocks. Press on the straight of the grain with a dry iron and avoid stretching any bias seams. Press most seams open to distribute the number of layers of fabric evenly. Use spray starch to persuade blocks into shape; however, if a block is too far out of square, rip it out or start over.

SHEENA J. NORQUAY's patchwork was inspired by the contours of the land and the movement of the wind. She quilted the design freehand, apart from penciled dots along the edges of the triangles where lines begin or end. Sheena quilted the small blue triangles using continuous radiating lines, then the large blue and large brown triangles using continuous radiating and contour lines.

▶ **Different ways of machine quilting a patchwork quilt**

Top: If the patches are cut accurately and sewn straight, you can stitch in the ditch to emphasize the graphic pattern. Stitching in the seam line requires accurately sewn intersections. **Center:** If the piece is stitched inaccurately, your options are limited to an all-over pattern or meandering. For this quilt, the patchwork is disregarded and free-motion quilted with a large-scale free-form pattern. **Below:** This pieced top has patches that are all the same size. A grid is stitched on point over the entire top.

Stitching order

To quilt a patchwork top you must work from the center to the outside edge of the quilt for each subsequent step.
1 Anchor the layers along the blocks, sashings, borders, and the very outer edge of the top.
2 Go back to the center and work outward, filling in large-scale details of the patchwork and any large motifs.
3 Begin in the center again, adding details to the motifs.
4 Begin in the center and add any background fillers.

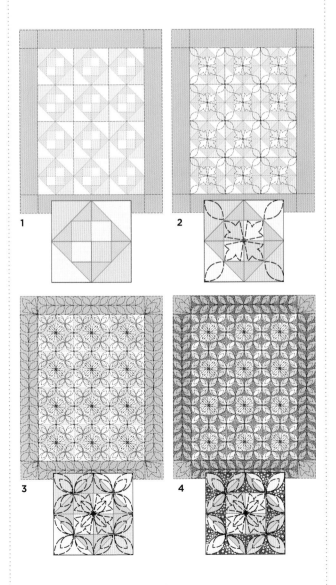

Planning for an appliqué quilt

Appliqué quilts may have large, open areas of fabric waiting to be filled with machine quilting, and how you choose to do this needs careful planning.

The main challenge when planning machine quilting for an appliqué top lies in the vast amount of empty background space that it is often necessary to fill. Measure the space the quilt will occupy and make a graph-paper plan for the finished size. Try out different quilting ideas until you find one that will best fill the background while also complementing the appliqué motifs. Remember to keep the quilting even throughout the entire quilt surface. Often simple geometric lines or grids are used to enhance a floral appliqué top.

Keep your plan interesting by dividing large empty spaces into sections that can be filled with beautiful quilting designs and background patterns. Create sections by drawing a border to compartmentalize spaces that would not exist without the decorative stitching.

Free-motion quilting works well to enhance the appliqué quilt. Stitching an outline in the ditch around the appliquéd shape and then flattening the background around the shape with a fill pattern will puff it out, allowing it to catch the light. Backgrounds can be filled with any of the tiny stipple patterns, grids, or echo quilting. Echoing around the design is an especially good choice to add emphasis without distraction by repeating the outline of the appliquéd shape.

The appliquéd motifs on this quilt, designed by JOANIE ZEIER POOLE, were followed with a line of quilting stitches on the background fabric, then the background was filled with spirals, mimicking the printed fabric.

Stitching order

Quilting an appliqué quilt follows the same progression as for any other quilt.
1 Anchor the layers of the quilt with a line of stitching around the edge of the central square and outer edge of the quilt.
2 Outline each appliqué shape with a line of stitching.
3 Stitch in the appliqués and the border fabric.
4 Fill the background.

1

2

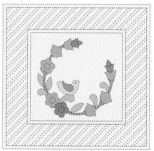

3

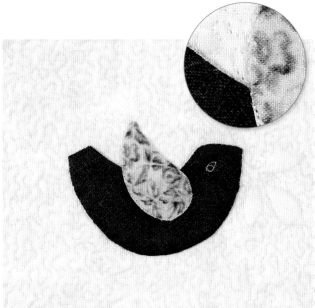

▲ **Types of quilting for an appliqué quilt**
Top left: The hand appliquéd bird is accentuated by the flattening of the background with tiny stippling. **Top right:** The bird is applied with mock hand appliqué by machine and outline quilted with invisible thread and then the background filled with hearts and loops, stitched with a variegated thread. **Bottom left:** This raw edge appliqué is finished with a buttonhole stitch, and a small area around the design is filled with tiny stippling to simplify the outline, while a grid fills the background. **Bottom right:** A tiny zigzag stitch secures the raw edge of this broidery perse block; leaves and flowers inspired by the fabric are quilted in the background with variegated thread.

Planning for a wholecloth quilt

Always a crowd-pleaser at museums and quilt shows, the wholecloth quilt is a tribute to the dimensional texture that can be achieved by the utilitarian task of holding the quilt layers with lines of stitching. In the past, these beauties took many hours, possibly even years of work, and can now be replicated in a fraction of the time when using machine quilting.

Here, a single motif plastic stencil (from the "Julia Elements Quilting Design Packet" by JOANIE ZEIER POOLE) was traced with a water-soluble marker to create a wholecloth layout. One motif in a wreath and border setting is surrounded by simple straight and scalloped lines. Notice that all of the lines and motifs have a double outline, allowing for the space around the motifs to be flattened with a background fill pattern.

When quilting a wholecloth quilt you have a wonderful opportunity to fill your layout with images that tell a story, or to include initials and dates that will last as a remembrance of any special occasion. For inspiration for your wholecloth layout, study the treasures from the past photographed for historical quilt books. Traditionally, the quilt surface was filled with a medallion, wreaths, garland-style borders, and grid backgrounds.

Plan to the final detail—all there is to look at is the design you plan. Search for images on the Internet, in books, and in designs left by artists of the past in wood and stone carvings, and jewelry. Adjust the size of the designs to fit your needs. Use traditional quilting designs or create a new tradition all your own.

Remember to fill the entire layout, including any background patterns that will need to be marked on the top. Transfer the small graph-paper layout to full-size drawings that will be used when tracing.

Taking building facades in New York City as inspiration, JERI RIGGS drew the major design lines on one wedge of a piece of white paper, folded the paper into eight wedges, then repeated eight times around the center to create this tie-dyed quilt.

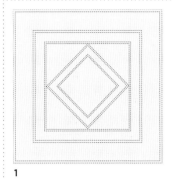
1

2

1

2

3

4

Stitching order

Stitching a wholecloth quilt follows the same method for anchoring as for any quilt. Begin each step in the center of the quilt and work toward the outside edge, keeping the quilting evenly distributed over the entire quilt.

1 First, anchor all straight lines, working from the center out, using a walking foot or a free-motion foot.

2 Using free-motion quilting, outline the largest motifs in all of the spaces, working from the center to the outer border.

3 Add the small details within the motifs.

4 Finally, fill with background fillers.

See how the design from JOANIE ZEIER POOLE is used to fill this wholecloth layout. The simple leaf and acorn motifs are used as a base for all of the designs. Coordinating block, setting triangle, and multisized borders fill the divisions of space created by simple double lines. To quilt this piece, anchor on the straight lines then, working from the center out, outline the largest motifs in all of the spaces, working from the center to the outer border. Go back and fill in small details and, finally, fill in the background if desired.

Choosing fabrics for the quilt top

Fabric makes up the largest component of the quilt. Choose good quality for best results and to honor the time you are investing in each project.

Quilters today can choose from an abundance of beautifully designed, high-quality fabric that will last through frequent washings. The quality has improved over the years with a higher thread count giving fabrics a luxurious feel. Most are colorfast and should shrink only slightly, if at all. Purchasing good fabric not only does your quilting work justice, but will also make your project go smoothly.

TYPES OF FABRIC
Today, as has been common for generations, most everyday quilts are made with 100% **cotton** fabric. This is a stable fiber that should not stretch when handled properly. Medium to lightweight are good choices; heavy drapery weight could be too stiff and heavy to sleep under, but is used for the wall or for decorating projects. Some cotton flannels are loosely woven and will stretch. Because they have a nice fluffy loft, the stitches are hidden, so use those for the quilt back.

If you choose to use other fiber contents, expect other characteristics. **Polyester** stretches. Some **silk** works beautifully and some is just too soft and slippery. If you really want to use a fine, lightweight fabric, line it with a layer of lightweight fusible interfacing.

Unless you are a seasoned pro, use the same weight of fabric throughout the quilt.

COLORED FABRICS
It is not only the scale of the print, but the colors of the fabrics you use that have an impact on your quilting stitches. Light colors reflect light, while dark colors absorb it and can swallow up the quilting design.

Consider where to show off quilting designs. Elegant quilting is often best shown on solid and almost solid fabrics. Keep in mind when choosing the solid fabrics that the value (darkness of color) will determine whether you need a light box to trace the pattern lines onto the fabric (see page 57). Robert Kaufman Fabrics offers cotton sateen in solid colors that have a wonderful sheen that will highlight the quilting designs.

Complementary colors look brighter when placed next to each other.

Bold color choices are featured in this quilt by JOANIE ZEIER POOLE and PAM LEVENHAGEN. Orange and blue are known as complementary colors because they sit opposite each other on the color wheel. When placed side by side, as in this quilt, the colors seem to vibrate.

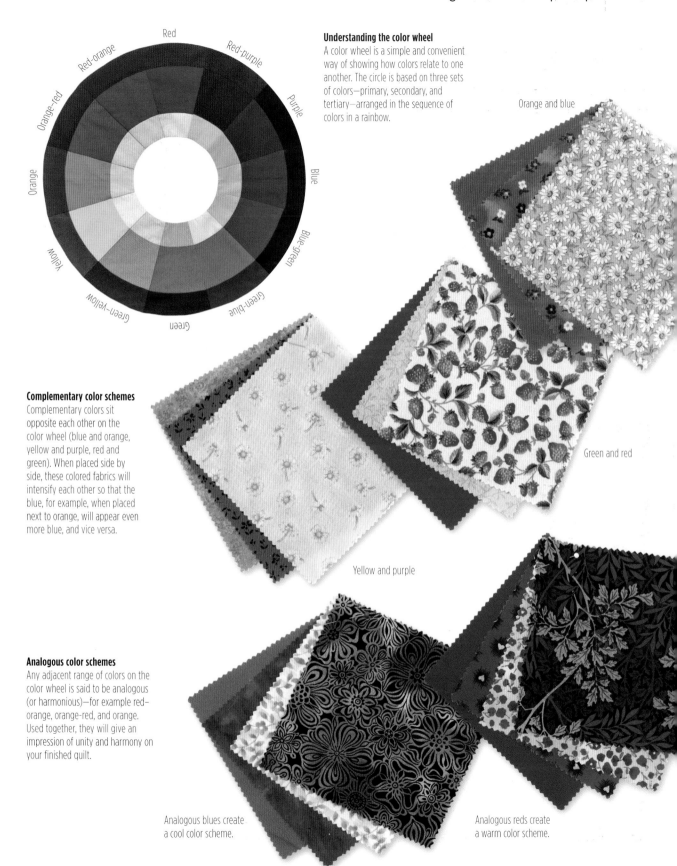

Red
Red-orange
Red-purple
Orange-red
Purple
Orange
Blue
Yellow
Blue-green
Green-yellow
Green-blue
Green

Understanding the color wheel

A color wheel is a simple and convenient way of showing how colors relate to one another. The circle is based on three sets of colors—primary, secondary, and tertiary—arranged in the sequence of colors in a rainbow.

Orange and blue

Complementary color schemes

Complementary colors sit opposite each other on the color wheel (blue and orange, yellow and purple, red and green). When placed side by side, these colored fabrics will intensify each other so that the blue, for example, when placed next to orange, will appear even more blue, and vice versa.

Green and red

Yellow and purple

Analogous color schemes

Any adjacent range of colors on the color wheel is said to be analogous (or harmonious)—for example red–orange, orange-red, and orange. Used together, they will give an impression of unity and harmony on your finished quilt.

Analogous blues create a cool color scheme.

Analogous reds create a warm color scheme.

PATTERNED FABRICS

When planning projects that include a large-scale print, choose the focus fabric first, then choose the blenders—the medium- to small-scale prints—solids, and almost solid fabrics based on the colors used within it. Large-scale prints may not look as nice when cut into little pieces; use those for larger spaces like the wide borders. However, keep in mind that fancy quilting designs may be hidden by busy fabrics, so, to save time, just quilt what the manufacturer printed.

Logic would tell you to put the largest prints in the largest spaces of the quilt. Find the spaces of the layout that can best highlight your quilting designs, then assign fabrics to those areas that show your efforts, possibly the borders, stripping, or larger sections of patchwork.

Focus   Solid   Blender   Solid   Blender   Blender

The focus fabric determines the color of both the blender and solid-color fabrics.

HOW MUCH FABRIC SHOULD I USE?

When you have finished planning which fabric goes where on your graph-paper layout, make a separate cutting plan on graph paper to determine how much of each fabric is needed. Drawing a cutting plan on graph paper is also a great idea if you haven't had a lot of experience with sewing. Draw the top and backing and allow extra space needed when cutting the bias strips for matching binding (see page 94). Add additional pieces needed when making more than one item and take your plan along when purchasing fabric for more assistance.

Buying extra fabric is always a good idea. It's there if you make a mistake, and if you don't use it in your quilt you can add it to your fabric stash. Having a stash is the sign of a true quilter.

Fabrics with sheen

When using sateen or any other fabric with sheen, keep in mind that it should be cut and assembled with the sheen running in the same direction. To keep pieces organized, place a pin to indicate the top of each piece when cutting.

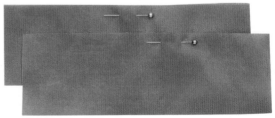

Fabric preparation

If you want to control a happy and mistake-free outcome for your work, you must pay close attention to the details. Preparing your fabrics correctly will save time and frustration in the long run. Following these fabric preparations is another step in keeping your standards high in every step of the process.

PREWASHING

It is important for machine quilters to take the time to prewash their fabrics. Since you will most likely want to be able to wash your quilt, you want each piece to be preshrunk and colorfast. Prewashing the fabrics should prevent any further bleeding or distortion due to shrinkage of individual fabrics.

Allow the fabric to soak in lukewarm water in a white sink or tub for a minute, one piece at a time. If a fabric bleeds, either don't use it, or soak it in a product that will set the dye permanently. If the fabric color does not run, wring excess water out in the spin cycle of the washer, partially dry the fabric in the dryer, then press it following the grain until completely dry. Next, fold the fabric to a convenient size for storage, and store away from light until ready to use.

PRESSING WITH SPRAY STARCH

Use any commercial spray starch, or mix your own—liquid starch and dry corn starch are available from grocery stores. The starch alternatives currently being sold in quilt stores do not seem to hold as well as the other products. There are a number of instances when spray starch is required:

• **At the beginning of a project, after the fabric has been prewashed and before you cut the first piece.** When you discover the benefits of stabilizing the fabric for cutting, you will never go back to cutting stretchy fabric with folds in it ever again! Starch only what you intend to use for the project and rinse out any excess before you put your fabric away for storage; it is a corn-based product that could attract bugs in certain climates.

• **During the assembly of each patch that goes into each patchwork block.** Develop a pressing plan for each block pattern used by making a practice block. Before opening the seam with the right sides facing, press each patch flat with a dry iron to set the seam and to avoid stretching. Then, press most seams open to distribute the number of

Meticulous pressing with the use of spray starch will stabilize the fabric so it will not stretch as you work.

layers of fabric evenly. As the patches are sewn together to make a block, use spray starch to persuade the blocks into shape. However, if a block is too far out of square, rip it out or start over.

• **When adding borders**, press the seams to one side, providing a low side of the gutter to follow along for stitch in the ditch.

• **After the top is assembled**, press all the seams from the back of the quilt and use spray starch to hold them in the chosen direction. Next, press the top from the front, checking to see that no folds have been pressed into the seams.

• **Before marking**, press a wholecloth top with a generous application of spray starch to avoid stretching during marking, basting, and quilting.

Cleaning your iron

Heat the iron to the lowest setting then turn it off. Rub away any starch residue on the iron with a terry towel dipped in white vinegar.

Press seams to one side where you wish to make a low side of the ditch for guiding the needle for stitch in the ditch. Press seams open where you wish to avoid bumping into a mountain of seams. This will evenly distribute the layers of fabric.

Backing fabric

A quilt's backing is the bottom layer of the quilt bundle, the fabric you see on the back of the quilt that keeps the batting inside. You might also hear the backing referred to as the "lining" or "the back."

BACKING FABRIC CHOICES

Reasons for choosing a particular fabric to use on the back of the quilt vary widely. You may choose something that is soft when placed against the skin, or your goal may be to use up some "ugly fabric" because it will always be hidden against a wall. Or you may spend many hours searching for the perfect pattern specifically chosen to show off your quilting stitches, because the back will be seen by the judges at a quilt show.

A firm, slightly stiffened backing fabric helps to prevent annoying puckers that occur when the fabric stretches during quilting. Resist the attraction to a bargain bin of cheaper-quality fabrics and sheets. Most quilt stores will sell high-quality fabrics that have languished on the shelves for too long at a reduced price. If you just can't resist stretchy, lightweight fabric, use an extra helping of starch to stabilize it.

Since the backing fabric is on the reverse of the quilt, it can be the perfect place to use up leftover fabric purchased for the quilt top. But keep the pieces to a minimum and as seam-free as possible, because seams hidden on the underside of the bundle can interrupt the stitching rhythm when you run into them unexpectedly. Be sure to press the seams open to evenly distribute the layers of fabric.

COLOR AND PATTERN

A busy fabric chosen for the backing will hide less-than-perfect quilting stitches. Whether the scale of the pattern is large or small, your stitching will be hidden in a multicolored backing fabric. A solid will show every stitch on the back, and is not a great choice for beginners. Unless you are very precise when assembling the layers, avoid stripes or patterns printed in straight rows that require perfect alignment of all layers.

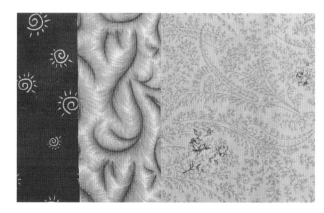

Suitable backing fabrics
These small-print fabrics are great choices for backing your quilt if you are not an experienced machine quilter and want your stitches to be hidden by the busy print.

Unsuitable backing fabrics
These fabrics make less desirable choices for the backing because the stripe and obvious geometric shapes printed in rows are difficult to align with the stitching on the top of the quilt.

HOW MUCH BACKING FABRIC SHOULD YOU BUY?

The amount of fabric to purchase for the backing will depend on two factors: the finished size of the top; and the width of the backing fabric. The easiest way to use a backing would be to cut it from a single piece of fabric, either regular quilting fabric, usually 41–44 in (104–112 cm) wide, or from wide yardage, which has a width that varies up to 108 in (274 cm). Many quilt shops and large chain fabric stores sell this wide yardage manufactured just for backing—an excellent choice if you find a printed pattern and color that suits your project.

Backings for small quilts can be cut from a single width of regular quilting fabric. To determine how much to buy, simply measure the length of the quilt top and add 4 in (10 cm) for some fabric to hold while quilting.

Backing for a larger quilt may need to be pieced in panels. If the total width needed is less than the width of the assembled backing, purchase two times the total length. If the quilt top total width is greater than the width of two assembled backing panels, purchase three total lengths for the backing.

A word of caution about fabric size

Many instructions for basting a quilt call for the backing fabric to be 4 in (10 cm) larger than the top on all sides, because of take-up that occurs during the quilting process. The same instructions will tell you to tape the backing layer to the work surface and just lay the batting and the top on the backing and baste. This not ideal. Having a backing that is so much larger than the top makes it difficult to secure the top edges with tape.

A better idea is to plan that both the top and backing are several inches larger than the desired finished size, not only for the take-up during the quilting process, but also to have a few extra inches to hold onto while quilting so you are not quilting out to the very edge of the quilt. Both layers of fabric need to be secured with tape when you baste and have even distribution of tension. Add the excess to all sides of the top and backing and if there is a loss of size (and there will be), lose it evenly throughout the quilt.

MEASURING FOR A MULTI-PANEL BACKING

After the quilt top is assembled and pressed you can accurately measure its size. Add an extra 1 in (2.5 cm) to all sides of the top and use that measurement for the backing fabric. If the size required is wider than one width of fabric, you will need to sew one or more panels together to get the required size.

1 Cut two or three fabric panels to the desired length. Trim off the selvage edges.

2 Sew the panels together using a 1/2 in (1.3 cm) seam allowance for stability.

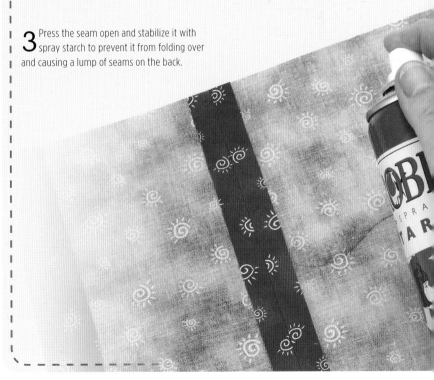

3 Press the seam open and stabilize it with spray starch to prevent it from folding over and causing a lump of seams on the back.

Marking for machine quilting

There are a number of ways to mark your fabric with lines to follow when stitching, bearing in mind of course that the lines need to be easily and thoroughly removed.

A world of possibilities opens up to you when you take the time to mark quilting motifs on your quilt top. Sometimes when you need to work fast you may not take the time to really plan well, or you may skip the marking process because it seems like a tedious task. But there are benefits to be gained from the time spent on marking. Marking lines is a valuable training exercise for the stitching phase of your projects since it helps to imprint the design in your brain, and tracing the design numerous times will help you understand how to navigate each design when it comes to actual stitching.

Useful marking tools are shown here (from top: white pencil, blue water-soluble markers, dressmaker's chalk, pounce pad with heat-release chalk). Avoid using ink, lead, and graphite markers as they will not wash out.

NAME	Blue water-soluble markers
HOW IT WORKS	Marks extensive designs on your quilts. If your designs are drawn on a computer, print them out onto paper, and trace the designs onto the fabric with a blue wash-away marker—using a light box, if it is necessary, to see the printed lines through the fabric.
ADVANTAGES	Easy-to-use, inexpensive, and readily available in quilt shops and large chain fabric stores. Shows up surprisingly well on most fabrics; it can also be used to mark with stencils too, if your fabric isn't too dark. Removes easily and consistently with cold water.
DISADVANTAGES	Only disadvantage is that the blue line may be difficult to see on blue or very dark fabrics. On the whole, though, blue markers are the first choice of many machine quilters.

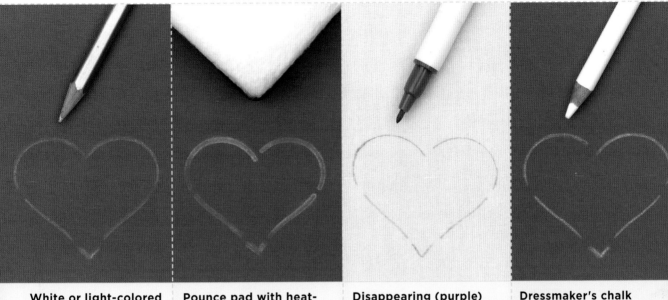

White or light-colored pencils

Perfect for marking dark fabrics. Available in erasable or water-soluble, in white, silver, and light colors. They may look like pencil encased in wood or be sold as a mechanical pencil with a package of replacement lead.

Easy to use with a plastic stencil or when tracing a pattern printed on paper on a light box.

Not for marking light-colored fabrics. The point of the pencil can break easily, especially when sharpening. If the color contains a high wax content, the line may be difficult to remove.

Pounce pad with heat-release chalk

Pad is filled with chalk and pressed in a swiping motion over a stencil that has been placed in position on the quilt top. Remove with a hot dry iron, a shot of steam from an iron, or a hair-dryer.

The improved heat-release powder stays on well. The chalk shows up well on dark or busy fabric. This may be a smart choice for people with hand difficulties. Easy to use with a plastic stencil or when tracing a pattern printed on paper on a light box.

The size of the motif is restricted to the size of the stencil and cannot be changed. If you are creating an heirloom piece that will not be washed often, bear in mind that the heat-release powder has not been on the market long enough for its long-term effects to be well-documented.

Disappearing (purple) marker

Contains ink that will disappear after 24 hours. The purple color shows up on most light-colored fabrics.

Has a fine line and can be used to add marking when needed during the quilting process.

May disappear with humidity before you have completed the quilting. If it is not washed out, it will leave chemicals in the fabric that have been known to reappear.

Dressmaker's chalk marker

Creates a light application of chalk, but often comes in the form of a pencil.

Easy to use and readily available at your local quilt store. New chalks have hit the market that have more staying power. Works well on dark fabrics.

Chalk may crumble and doesn't always wash out.

WHEN TO MARK

Marking is done after the top is assembled and accurately pressed and stabilized, but before it is basted. The top should be pressed with spray starch until it is flat and stable. The spray starch will prevent the fabric from stretching during the marking and machine quilting processes.

Always do a practice drive with a quilting design before you add it to your layout. You may decide to alter the design before you trace it onto the quilt with modifications that simplify it by eliminating some details, or you may find you need to connect areas for continuous stitching.

MARKING METHODS

There are many ways to mark the fabric, using various tools. Experiment to find which work best for your project and you. Your choices include using markers or pencils to trace a stencil or a design printed on paper. You can mark straight lines with masking tape (available in various widths). The motif can be drawn on a piece of quilting paper that you pin to the quilt, stitch through, then tear away. You can draw around objects, or use stencils designed for accurately tracing straight lines or grids. Use a circle stencil from an office supply store to invent a multitude of designs based on that simple shape.

MARKING WITH A WATER-SOLUBLE MARKER

Blue water-soluble markers are the first choice of many machine quilters because they are so easy to use with a plastic stencil or when tracing a design printed on paper. They provide an accurate line that is removed easily and consistently with cold water.

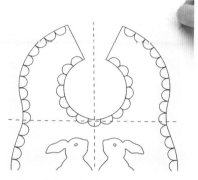

1 For a design printed on paper, tape the paper pattern to the work surface.

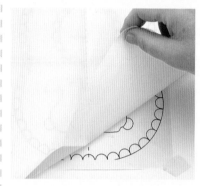

2 Fold the fabric in half in both directions and gently crease it. Center the fabric over the design and tape the edges to stop it from slipping.

3 Mark the design on the fabric with a water-soluble marker. Never iron a quilt top that has been marked with this marker, since the heat sets the ink permanently.

TRACE AND STITCH MARKING

A method chosen when the fabric is dark or multicolored, or cannot get wet, is to mark the design on a special quilting paper. This lightweight tracing paper, manufactured by Golden Threads, is available in long rolls, and is durable enough to stitch through, but can easily be removed.

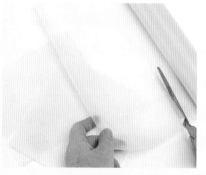

1 Cut a piece of Golden Threads quilting paper large enough on all sides to avoid the design when pinning it to the quilt surface.

2 Lay a printed design on the work surface. Place the paper over the printed design and trace it with any quilting pencil or marker.

USING A POUNCE PAD

Some quilters use a pounce pad for marking dark or multicolored fabrics. The plastic holder is filled with heat-release chalk that dispenses from a terry cloth pad when rubbed over a stencil positioned on the quilt top.

1 Center the stencil on the quilt top. Use masking tape, if you need to, to keep the stencil from sliding.

2 Slide the pounce pad over the design.

3 The image will be printed on the fabric. When the quilting is complete, the chalk will disappear with the heat of an iron. Be sure to wash the quilt after removing the chalk.

Using a light box

If your fabric is too dark to easily see a printed design through it, tape the paper design to the lighted surface of a light box. Carefully center the fabric over the paper design and tape it down to avoid slipping. Trace the design with a light-colored pencil.

3 Pin the quilting paper in place on the quilt with a few straight pins.

4 Stitch through the paper and quilt bundle, following the traced lines.

5 Gently pull the paper away from the stitches, using caution not to pull on the stitches. Remove all of the paper fragments before any background quilting is stitched.

Batting

A lofty layer of batting makes a quilt fluffy, warm, and enduring. Take a close look at the battings that are available, and determine which are best for your different machine quilting tasks.

Over the years, the center layer of a quilt may have been anything from newspaper to horsehair to articles of worn-out clothing. You may remember thick carded wool quilts that were difficult to care for. Nowadays, quilters have an abundance of wonderful batting materials to choose from, from natural fibers to manmade synthetics to environmentally sound choices.

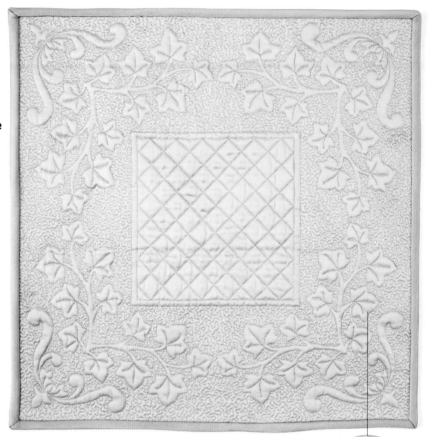

A high-loft batting adds a three-dimensional quality to this Ivy Wreath design by JOANIE ZEIER POOLE, filling the leaves and scrolls attractively.

A note on wool batting

Many machine quilters have come to realize that using wool batting has been a huge factor in the success of their work. It not only makes the job easier, its loft fills the quilted motifs so they catch the light, making the extra process of trapunto (see page 90) unnecessary to add fullness to the designs.

Purchase only 100% wool that is completely washable and is manufactured to resist bearding. This ³/₈ in (9 mm) thick batting is wonderfully full-bodied yet compresses nicely to flatten backgrounds, and then springs back to fill the quilting designs. It is also lightweight, making the quilt bundle weigh significantly less, which makes it a delight to work with when maneuvering a large quilt in the small space of the machine.

CHOOSING AN APPROPRIATE BATTING

Manufacturers offer a wide selection of batting, and your choice will depend on how the quilt will be used. If you are making a decorative art quilt for the wall you have different priorities when choosing supplies than when you make a quilt to drape a bed. There are options available to make items to decorate the home, protect a table with a runner using heat-resistant batting, insulate cold, drafty windows with insulated batting, or make clothing that is lightweight, pliable, and not bulky.

READ THE INFORMATION PRINTED ON THE BAG

The bag that contains the batting has a more important function than to just protect the batting during shipping. It details the batting specifications and care information. The size, weight, fiber content, and handling instructions are there to assist you in your decision on which is the best choice for your project. You will also find information regarding how far apart you need to space the stitching so the batting does not fall apart, as well as what shrinkage you should expect from washing.

SHRINKAGE

As with any batting, plan for some shrinkage from washing. If you absolutely do not want the batting to shrink after you have quilted your piece, wash it before you use it. Follow manufacturers care instructions. And remember: the more quilting you do, the smaller your quilt will become.

▶ Types of batting

1 Wool: 100% super washed wool blended with binder fibers to bond the soft and natural fiber. Wool is the ultimate for machine quilting due to its airy loft that returns to original condition when squished in the small space of the machine head. This batting weighs significantly less than any other batting (except silk) which makes it easy to maneuver the bundle, even with a large quilt. It is soft and drapes well on a bed and hangs flat on a wall. Shrinkage 0–3%. Stitch spacing up to 4 in (10 cm).

2 White cotton: 100% bleached cotton. This traditional batting is used by machine quilters, who get a puckered, antique look by washing the quilt after completing the quilting. It is stiffer and heavier than wool, and does not have the loft. Used with very light fabrics. Needle punched for strength with a stitching area as much as 8–10 in (20–25 cm) apart.

3 Natural cotton: 100% natural cotton. Same as white cotton. Needle punched for strength. Shrinkage is 3–5%. Stitch distance is 8–10 in (20–25 cm) apart.

4 Cotton/polyester blend (80/20%): Very clean cotton, natural color. It is stiffer and heavier than wool, large quilts will need to be rolled during the quilting process. The loft is low but will show some definition when quilted. Shrinkage is 3–5%. Stitch distance is 8–10 in (20–25 cm) apart. Needle punched for lightweight support without stiffness.

5 Soy/cotton blend (50/50%): Soy protein fiber is eco-friendly and truly friendly to skin. It is comfortable, drapes well, and does not retain a crease, making this soft, very thin batting a good choice for miniatures, clothing, or any lightweight project. Shrinkage 2–3%. Stitch distance is up to 8–10 in (20–25 cm) apart.

6 Polyester fleece: Densely constructed polyester provides a sturdy batting for home decorating projects like table runners and placemats. This batting is not recommended for heirloom quilts since the manmade fibers are slippery, causing the quilt layers to shift, and it may migrate through dark fabrics. Polyester traps body warmth and moisture. Shrinkage 0–2%. Stitch distance 4 in (10 cm).

Pin pointers

By cutting the batting 1 in (2.5 cm) smaller than the top, you will avoid having that annoying fluffy edge of batting to catch on the needle and foot every time you need to slide the bundle in and out.

•

For an everyday quilt, you can piece together large batting pieces—this is not recommended for an heirloom. Cut the edges to be joined very straight. Butt the edges; do not overlap. Use a herringbone stitch by hand or a blind hem by machine to join the pieces.

1

2

3

4

5

6

Basting the layers

Before you machine quilt, you must baste the layers together to prevent them from shifting, which will cause puckering during the quilting process. Learn about the different methods and which is the best choice for your project.

Basting is the final preparatory step before you begin to quilt. It is done after the top and backing have had their final pressing with spray starch and the quilting designs have been marked on the top.

IMPORTANT CONSIDERATIONS
Machine quilters have different considerations when holding the layers together temporarily during the quilting process. Basting with thread, as you may do for hand quilting, is not recommended because once the thread is driven over with quilting stitches it is difficult to remove. The exception to this is to use a water-soluble thread that will wash away when the quilting is

complete, or to hire a longarm quilter to baste using washaway thread in the top of the machine and in the bobbin.

FINDING A SUITABLE WORK SURFACE
The options for basting that we will cover include pinning the layers with safety pins, spray basting, basting on a table, and using a basting frame. The method you choose will vary depending on the size of each project. The work surface you need depends on the size of your quilt and may determine how (un)comfortable you will be as you baste. Think about this phase of the project in advance if your space is limited: can you handle a large basting project in your home? Be on the look

out for a location you might have access to for the basting process. Ask to use a large work area in the home of a friend, or at a community center.

Choose a work surface that is a comfortable height when standing. Basting on a counter-height surface is best for your back. If the piece is too large for the counter, you can baste it in sections, securing the center section first, then working on each side. Use the clamps available for holding a picnic tablecloth or bulldog-style clips from an office supply store to secure the layers along the sides, and use masking tape to hold the ends if the clips won't reach the quilt edge.

PIN BASTING A SMALL QUILT
A small quilt can easily be pin basted on a table or counter. Tiny gold safety pins are perfect for the job and don't get in your way. Large safety pins will get in your way when maneuvering a small piece under the machine head.

1 Secure the backing fabric to the work surface, wrong side up, with masking tape. Use caution not to stretch any of the layers when basting. Place a piece of masking tape at each corner and every 8 in (20 cm) along each side.

2 Smooth the batting on top of the backing.

Pin pointers

Some quilters need to use the floor for basting large quilts. Use knee pads for hard surfaces and work for short periods of time. When working on carpet, slide a cutting mat under the bundle so you don't pin to the carpet.

- Straight quilting pins can be used for small projects that will not be transported before the process is complete. Follow the same process as for safety pins.

Use masking tape to hold the ends if they do not reach the table edge.

BASTING ON A BANQUET-STYLE TABLE

Push two banquet-style tables together for large quilts, using masking tape or clamps for all edges. Protect with a cutting mat so the pins don't scratch the surface. Bring the table up to a comfortable height by adding four bed-height extenders or sections of PVC pipe under the legs.

Hold all three layers securely with bulldog clips or picnic table clamps. You may need about 400–500 pins for a queen-sized quilt. Baste the center section of the quilt first, then move it to one side, readjust the clips, baste, then do the final section.

3 Center the top over the first two layers and use tape to hold it down securely. Place a piece of masking tape over each piece from the backing layer. These strips of tape may need to be longer to reach the work surface or can be turned perpendicular to the edge of the quilt.

4 Pin baste every 4–5 in (10–12.5 cm), starting from the center and working outward. Avoid the placement of pins on the marked lines and anchor seams whenever possible. Finish by placing pins along the outer edges, then gently remove the tape from all the layers, taking care not to ravel the fabric edge.

Using a basting frame

In years past, quilting bees basted on a frame made from four long strips of wood supported by four chairs and held together at the corners with clamps. The quilt layers were held to the wood frame with thumbtacks or pinned to strips of fabric attached to the wood. This system can be a great way to pin-baste any quilt larger than a tabletop. The individual layers are attached to the frame one at a time with straight pins. Safety pins are placed throughout the quilt top, working from the outside of the quilt in as far as you can reach easily. Then the clamps are released and the quilt can be rolled to be made smaller and the pinning continues until the entire top is basted.

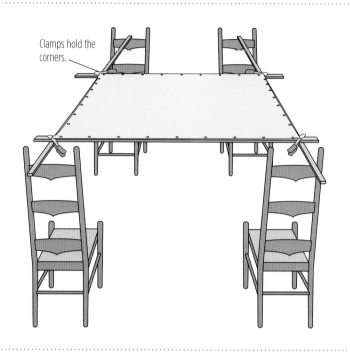

Clamps hold the corners.

USING BASTING SPRAY

Cover a table or floor with newspapers or a disposable tablecloth. Depending on how small the quilt is, spray all or half of the backing at a time. Follow the same steps for a larger piece, working in quarter sections if necessary.

1 Tape the backing to the work surface, wrong side up.

2 Lightly spray the backing with the basting spray, avoiding the outer edge if the batting is cut smaller.

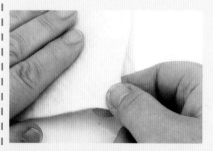

3 Center the batting on the backing and smooth it, pressing it to the backing.

4 Lightly spray the top of the batting. Center the quilt top on the batting and smooth out any wrinkles.

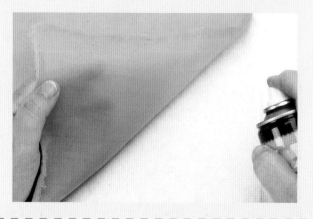

Threads

The world of thread has grown well beyond the choices of the past. Color, weight, fiber content, even the type of spool it is wound on have changed, and all play an important role in determining the success of any project.

There is no other way to begin this section other than to say, don't even think about using bargain thread to do this work. With the time you are investing in learning machine quilting and the time devoted to working on the project, you need good thread. High-quality thread is worth every penny and eliminates problems that the cheap brands can create. Purchase it from your local quilt store or at a quilt show directly from the manufacturer. Spend time with a representative to learn about all of their products, find out what will work best for your needs, and why they have developed so many choices.

You should choose the thread for each project based on what the quilt will be used for. Consider whether you need durability, or if the quilting line is merely decorative. Do you want the thread to show or hide? Are you adding color or detailed stitching to the piece?

THREAD COLOR

Choose the thread color depending on whether you want it to show up or hide. The stronger the contrast between the thread color and the fabric, the more the stitching will show. Consider your ability to stitch an accurate line before you choose a thread that has a high contrast to the fabric.

Thread used for fine machine quilting on solid fabric is often chosen to match the background fabric, hiding in the shadows and allowing the motifs to pop. If an exact match cannot be found, choose a darker shade. It will blend with the fabric color and hide slight variances in your stitching from the marked line.

Variegated thread is available in various weights of cotton or polyester for machine quilting. It can be chosen to either contrast or blend with the fabrics. It is a great choice for quilting a patchwork top or multicolored print fabric.

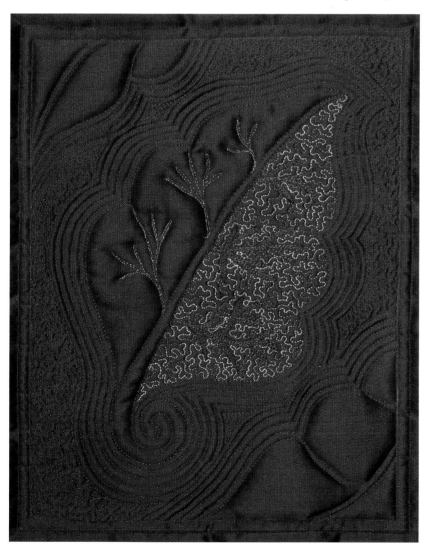

Several styles and colors of thread were used to create this vibrant art quilt by JOANIE ZEIER POOLE. Silk, polyester, metallic, and variegated threads in various weights outline, fill, and accentuate the leaf shapes.

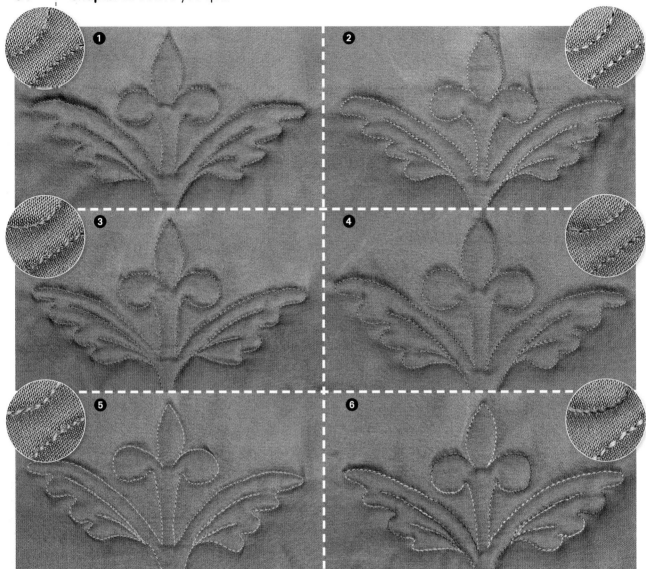

▲ Thread types

1 Polyester invisible thread is soft and subtle. Available in "clear" for quilting light-colored fabrics and "smoke" for more colorful fabrics, it hides on the fabric for quilting a multicolored patchwork top and can be used for invisible appliqué by machine. Invisible thread can get old and turn brittle.

2 Silk is a strong natural fiber. It is available in 50 and 100 weights. Heirloom machine quilters prefer the 100 wt/2-ply, which can be used in the top and in the bobbin of a machine. This thread works well for very tiny stitching necessary for micro-stippling and intricate designs. Silk transforms dull cotton fabric and its sheen is a perfect match for elegant silk or sateen fabric.

3+4 Polyester is a manmade fiber available in several weights. Example **3** was stitched with a 60 wt/2-ply polyester that can be used in the top of the machine for heirloom machine quilting, and in the bobbin. Heavier weights, like the 40 wt/3-ply used in **4**, are chosen for more utilitarian machine stitching, or if the stitching is intended to show.

5 100% cotton is available in many weights, from a durable heavyweight 30 to extra fine 100. This example was stitched with 50 wt/2-ply in the top and bobbin. It is lighter than regular sewing thread, which makes it a good choice to retrace and stipple without an unsightly build-up of thread.

6 Variegated threads are available for quilters in cotton, rayon, and polyester. This example is stitched with 40 wt/3-ply polyester. These threads look very different on the spool than when stitched, so stitch a sample to see if it looks like what you expected before using it on your quilt.

THREAD WEIGHT

Thread weight might be the most important factor in choosing thread for machine quilting. Does it need to be strong? Do you want it to be seen or to be hidden? Above all, your choice for the weight of thread should be based on the durability needed.

Thread labels can be confusing. While the labels display the weight and number of plies, the sizing is not an industry standard; it varies between companies. Generally, however, the higher the number, the finer the weight. 100 is very lightweight and 2-ply should be lighter weight than 3-ply.

- Use a durable **heavyweight thread,** 30 or 40 weight, for a really heavily used quilt. If the quilting designs are large and intended to draw attention, use heavier thread in a color that contrasts with the fabric, maybe variegated. If heavier thread is used for tiny, dense stitching, the quilt surface becomes cluttered with thread, which is objectionable.

- **Lightweight thread** should be used if you are making an heirloom piece with tiny stitching. The weight of the thread affects the length of your stitch. Many designs used for machine quilting require that the same line be stitched more than once. When fine or invisible thread is used, a line of stitching can be retraced without an unsightly build-up of thread. Using lightweight thread allows you to form tiny stitches that make up curved lines for motifs and for stippling.
- **Superior Threads'** Bottom Line, a 60-weight, lint-free polyester thread, is suitable for heirloom machine quilting and for piecing. It is available in a wide variety of colors, on large spools, is reasonably priced, and can be used in the top of the machine as well as the bobbin.

BOBBIN THREAD

We are asking our machines to perform at their best, and we have to do everything we can to support our partnership. In order for the machine to make perfect stitches, you must use bobbins that are made specifically for your machine by the manufacturer. Take the time to fill the bobbin evenly; you can not expect perfectly formed stitches and perfect tension if the bobbin is not filled correctly. Watch the bobbin while filling. Fill at half speed. Guide the thread with your hand if necessary to fill in neatly stacked rows.

Use a lightweight thread in the bobbin to match either the top fabric or the backing fabric. Several different colors may be used for the same quilt if desired.

Stacked or cross-wound spools

The way the manufacturer winds the thread on the spools (stacked or cross-wound) indicates the placement of the spool on your sewing machine.

Stacked

- The thread is wound around the spool continuously in straight rows stacked on top of one another. It is intended to unwind in the same way as it is wound onto the spool— from the side, not from the end. It does not matter if the thread unwinds from the front or back of the spool.
- Intended to stand up on the vertical pin on top of your machine.
- The spool can freely rotate.
- Thread unwinds straight from the side directly into the thread path without any waves or curls.
- If the thread works well when positioned on the horizontal spool pin, there is no need to change it to the vertical pin spool holder.

Cross-wound

- The spool is long and narrow, with the thread crisscrossing the spool.
- Intended to lie down on the horizontal spool pin.
- Designed to unwind from over the top end of the spool.
- The spool stays stationary.
- Use a spool cap to keep it from sliding off the spool pin.
- Use a free-standing thread stand if you only have a vertical spool pin and you want to use a cross-wound spool.

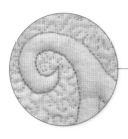

From the front, this quilt top is beautifully quilted using a harmonious lightweight cotton thread...

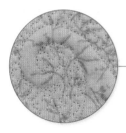

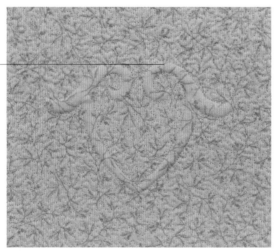

....but the back of a quilt is equally important, especially if you are submitting it for a competition or if you intend to show it off.

Pin pointer
When using lightweight or invisible thread, a thread stand may be necessary to achieve the proper tension. The thread stand stabilizes the thread and elevates it higher than the machine, allowing it to enter the thread path without added tension.

Get the most out of your bobbin thread
- Buy a lot of bobbins for your machine and thread all of your bobbins in commonly used colors before you start a project. There is nothing worse than breaking your concentration by having to stop in the middle of a project and thread your bobbin again.
- If your machine does not have an empty bobbin sensor, check the thread supply in the bobbin before you take off for a long stretch of quilting.
- If you unexpectedly run out of bobbin thread, you will need to lock the stitches. Begin the new thread at a nearby intersection if possible, then stitch right over the unsecured threads.
- Keep track of matching bobbins filled with a specific thread by using a pipe cleaner to keep them attached to one another.

COMMON FAULTS
- If you really want to use a slippery thread like rayon, use a thread net to keep it from falling off the spool.
- Lightweight threads create special requirements of the operation of your machine. If the thread is fraying and breaking, there may be a snag somewhere along the thread path. For this problem, you must take your machine in to get it checked.
- Thread breakage can be caused by using a needle that is too small, causing friction on the thread.
- Never use hand quilting thread in your machine; it has a coating that has been known to cause problems with the machine mechanism.
- Machine manufacturers warn us to never use invisible thread in the bobbin as it can wear a groove in the metal of the machine.

HOW MUCH THREAD SHOULD I USE?
The process of machine quilting uses a lot of thread, be sure to have a sufficient supply on hand.

	Light quilting	Medium quilting	Heavy quilting
Lap/crib size	400 yd (368 m)	800 yd (732 m)	1,200 yd (1,000 m)
Twin size	600 yd (549 m)	1,200 yd (1,000 m)	1,600 yd (1,463 m)
Queen size	800 yd (732 m)	1,000 yd (914 m)	2,000 yd (1,823 m)

Needles

The machine needle chosen for each project varies depending on the size and type of thread, not the sewing application.

The majority of machine quilters use a sharp needle in their machine; others choose a topstitch style. Needles are shown enlarged here so that you can make comparisons.

Standard sharp needle

Titanium-coated needle

Topstitch needle

SHARP NEEDLE

The sharp needle has a slim shaft and a very tapered sharp point. Use it to achieve smooth, even stitching on lightweight fabrics. The dainty size 60/8 is fragile and breaks easily. Size 70/10 is a better choice for newer quilters using lightweight thread. Sharp needles are the favorites of heirloom machine quilters who value the tiny hole left in the fabric and the lack of thread pop-ups from the bobbin.

TOPSTITCH NEEDLE

The topstitch needle has a larger, elongated eye and a deeper, wider groove that protects the thread. This is especially beneficial for delicate, decorative, and sensitive threads. The point is described as a light, sharp point that separates the fabric fibers, then penetrates (it does not have a razor sharp point that cuts). Consider using these when using heavier fabrics and some specialty threads.

TITANIUM-COATED NEEDLES

Titanium-coated needles cost more per needle than a regular needle, and the manufacturer states they last five to eight times longer than an uncoated needle.

RECOMMENDED SIZES

70/10	for very fine threads	(60 wt and finer)
80/12	for fine threads	(50 wt threads such as cotton, cotton/poly, silk)
90/14	for medium threads	(40 wt threads such as variegated, cotton and embroidery threads)
100/16	for heavier threads	(30 wt and heavier)

Needle know-how

- The size of the needle is etched into the shank. If you have a loose needle, check the shank to find the size.
- Needles can be defective right out of the package. A brand new needle can have a burr or could be slightly bent. If you experience problems like skipped stitches after installing the new needle, change it again to see if a defective needle could be the problem.
- Breaking a needle can scratch the needle plate. If there is a burr, it may snag the thread and cause breakage. Take it in for a repair or sand slightly with very fine sandpaper.

Pin pointer

Needles should be replaced after eight hours of stitching. Since you may quilt in snippets of time, here is a good reminder to change the needle. Fill three bobbins for a large project: when you have used up three bobbins, change the needle.

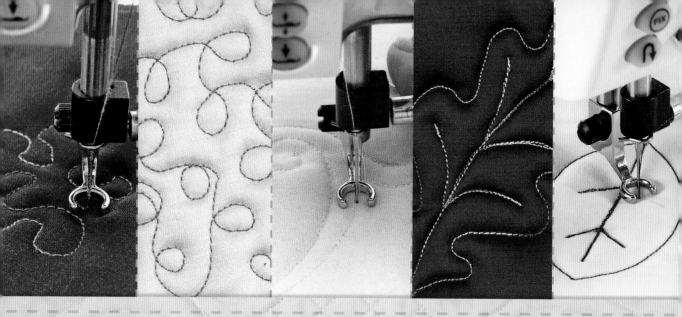

CHAPTER 3
Techniques

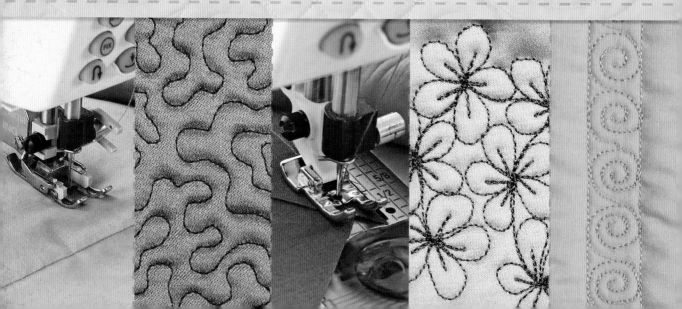

So far you have learned to plan and prepare your quilt bundle, but actually sitting down at the machine and beginning to stitch can be overwhelming. In this chapter we discuss how to adjust your machine to achieve perfect tension, how to travel from place to place, quilt in straight lines, and echo quilt, as well as how to use the free-motion foot to create myriad background fillers for your quilt projects. You can then complete your project by removing starch and markings, squaring up the quilted piece, and attaching a bias binding.

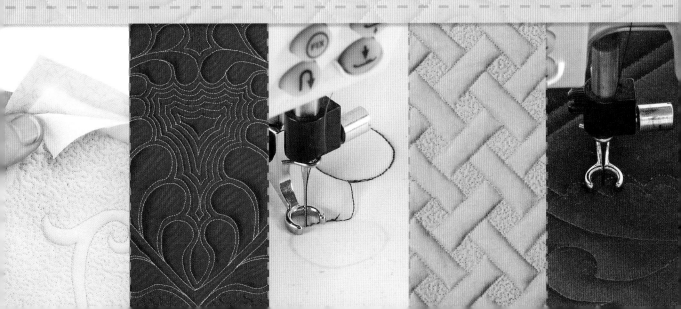

Starting to stitch your quilt

Completing your quilted projects with machine quilting will be easy when you understand how to take control of the bundle and the sewing machine. Use a practice bundle for the exercises on the next few pages, before taking the first stitch in your project.

HANDLING A LARGE QUILT BUNDLE

Working with a large quilt for machine quilting can be challenging. The best method for you may depend on your work space set-up or the size and strength of your body. Whether you use one of the methods described here, or invent your own, it is imperative that the area of the quilt you are working is kept flat against the bed of the machine. If you struggle when maneuvering the bundle, remember that anchoring is the only time during the quilting process that you will need to rotate the entire piece.

Puddling
When working on a large quilt you may benefit from having your quilt "puddled" on a table large enough to support the weight of the entire piece. Place the machine at the right side of a surface that is large enough to support the weight of the entire quilt, about 10 in (25 cm) back from the front edge. Place an additional surface (possibly a set of rolling drawers) to the left of your chair to provide additional support if needed.

Rolling the quilt
Some quilters roll or fold the quilt bundle, securing it with bicycle clips and throwing the roll over their shoulder. This works well for some but feels awkward for others. Rolling the quilt limits your access to the entire surface, and refolding the bundle takes time.

POSITIONING YOUR HANDS ON THE QUILT

How you position your hands on the quilt may change with the various stitching techniques needed to complete a project. Use the grip that provides the best control in each situation, and find a position that allows your elbows, wrists, and shoulders to relax.

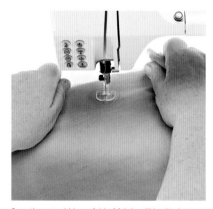

Sometimes, grabbing a fold of fabric will be the best way to slide the bundle across the bed of the machine.

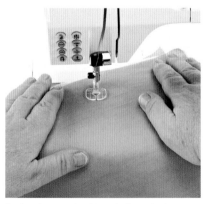

At other times your hands may be flat against the fabric.

Stitching secrets

- With stitching possible in any direction, you may wonder which way to stitch; forward or backward? Most often, you will want to stitch away from yourself. Think of it as driving a car: the open road is out in front of you.
- If your machine has a needle up/down setting, set it to the down position so that the needle will alway return to hold the layers when you stop stitching.
- Keep your hands on the bundle when the machine is running. If you pause or stop, keep your hands on the fabric until the needle is down.

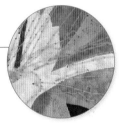

Self-taught machine quilter LAURA GLASS' best advice for beginners of free-motion stitching is to: "Relax and let your project flow through the machine. Think of the needle as a pen drawing. This can be easier said than done at first." For this quilt, Laura practiced on quilt "sandwiches" of fabric and batting to get a feel for the rhythm of the stitching. Outlining the main motifs, such as these lilies, is one way to anchor the quilt bundle before quilting individual areas of the motif and background.

The quilt stitching is used to add form and depth to the fabric flowers.

MOVING THE QUILT BUNDLE

If the quilt bundle feels tightly gripped under the pressure foot, first make sure the feed dogs are lowered. If the problem persists, there may be too much pressure on the presser foot. Check the owner's manual to see if the pressure can be adjusted.

Alternatively, it may be that the bed of your machine is not slick, in which case you may benefit from using the Supreme Slider, a Teflon sheet designed to cling to the machine bed and eliminate friction under the bundle. It is available at major quilt shows, quilt stores, and at www. freemotionslider.com.

Place the Supreme Slider on the bed of the machine, aligning the opening with the hole of the stitch plate.

The Teflon sheet miraculously clings to the bed of the machine and helps the bundle glide easily.

LOCKING THREAD ENDS

Thread ends need to be held securely at the beginning and end of each line of stitching, without being noticed. To do this, bring the bobbin thread to the top of the fabric as you lock the thread end, to avoid a bird's nest on the quilt back. To practice locking and stitching, layer two 18-in (46-cm) squares of muslin and batting held together with 16 pins. Install a needle sized to your thread and a free-motion foot, and lower the feed dogs.

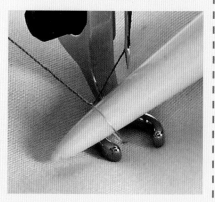

1 Determine where you want the first stitch to be. Begin with the needle in the uppermost position, hold on to the top thread, and insert the needle.

2 Rotate the fly wheel one entire turn, stopping with the needle at its highest position. You can do this by turning the fly wheel by hand, or by tapping the foot pedal once to lower and again to raise the needle. Alternatively, if you have a needle up/down button, push it once for down and once again to bring the needle up.

3 Tug on the top thread to bring the bobbin thread up, so you can pull it through to the top of the fabric. Slide a stiletto under the needle or use right-angle tweezers to grasp the bobbin thread.

4 Return the needle into the same hole in the fabric. Hold both threads out of the line of stitching and make six tiny locking stitches very close together. These stitches should occupy less than $1/4$ in (6 mm) of space. Stitch 2–3 in (5–7.5 cm) away from the locking stitches using your normal free-motion stitch length, stop with the needle down, and take your foot off the pedal. Clip the beginning thread ends at the surface of the quilt, as shown. Begin stitching again. When you come to the end of the line of stitching make another six locking stitches very close together. This will hold the thread securely and you can trim away the thread ends.

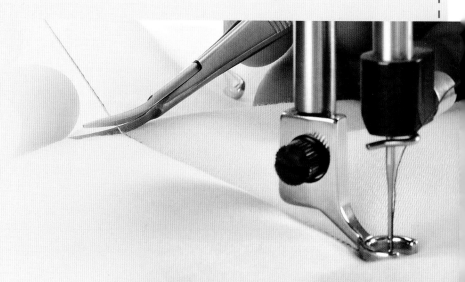

A note on stitch length

- For locking the stitches with the feed dogs up and the walking foot attached, set the stitch length to 0.5 for the locking stitch length and 1.5 to 3.0 for your regular stitch length—depending on the weight of the thread.
- For free-motion locking stitches with the feed dogs lowered, you will determine the stitch length by the distance you move the quilt before the machine takes another stitch. You are trying to attain a stitch length of 0.5 for locking and 1.5 to 3.0 for your regular stitch length.

Pin pointer
You may need to make adjustments to the height of your chair and your lighting to ensure you can see the area you need to drive to without extending your neck.

TESTING THE THREAD TENSION

Lightweight, metallic, and invisible threads can present tension problems, yet we have all admired how some people use these threads successfully, with wonderful results. You need to understand that when your machine was manufactured, it was most likely calibrated for perfect tension with 40 weight, 3-ply thread.

1 Stitch a straight line, stop, and look at the top and the back of the bundle to check the stitch quality. If the threads are catching one another correctly, both will look like a row of tiny, rounded bumps. Make a note of the thread weight and the original tension setting next to the stitching.

Correct thread tension. Threads catch one another in the middle of the layers.

Top tension is too tight; bobbin too loose. Reduce top tension or thread the hole in the bobbin case if you have one.

Top tension is too loose; bobbin tension is too tight. Increase top tension; reduce bottom tension.

2 Continue practicing some loops and zigzags. Changing the direction of the stitching lines can alert you to necessary adjustments needed. If either thread is straight, pulling the other thread to its side of the fabric, the tension is too strong and needs adjusting. Reduce the tension on it or increase the other thread tension, or both. When the tension has been adjusted correctly for a specific thread, write the settings and the thread description on the fabric next to the stitching.

3 Try stitching your name, it is imprinted in your brain and should be a familiar path.

4 Now test your machine tension with a different weight thread. If necessary, follow the tension guide to make adjustments.

Getting from place to place

Now that the tension is perfect, it is time to learn a few skills that will be used over and over when moving from one area of a layout to another with free-motion quilting.

When sitting at the machine, remember to focus on the direction you are moving toward, not on the needle, which will always stitch in exactly the same place. Look ahead at the stitching line to know where you are stitching next. When you need to pause or stop, keep your hands on the bundle until you take your foot off the pedal and the needle is down to hold the fabric.

Vary the speed of the machine depending on the difficulty of the design. Stitch at a speed at which you can comfortably stay on the lines—even if it is slow, this is not a race. Slowing down when you come to a curve or busy intersection allows you to concentrate on following the line more accurately. Place each stitch exactly where you want it and add speed as you learn to gain control of the stitching line.

RETRACING
Retracing is the term used when a line of stitching covers a section of a line that has already been stitched once. For instance, if the design contains a leaf, the center vein may be stitched from the base to the tip and then the line is followed back down to the base and on to the next leaf. Keep your eye on the previously stitched line and guide the needle exactly over the top of the first stitches.

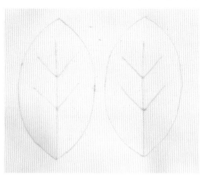

1 Draw several leaves on a practice bundle.

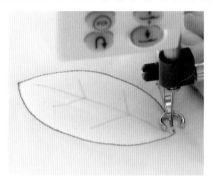

2 Start at the base of the leaf and stitch the entire outline, returning to the base without breaking the thread.

JUMP STITCHING
Using a jump stitch is another helpful way to travel if the new area to be stitched is not too far away.

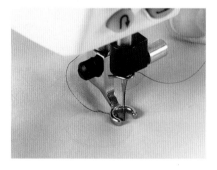

1 Draw several circles on a practice bundle and lock your thread on the outline of the first circle.

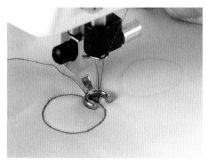

2 Stitch around the circle to just past the beginning locking stitches, then lock the thread again.

More ways to travel

There may be times when you can travel to a new area of stitching along the outer edge of the quilt without ending and beginning a new thread (1). Be sure that the stitching line is in an area that will be hidden by the binding. You can also travel between unconnected motifs using a line of stippling or another background filler. In example 2, each leaf was outlined and its details added before stitching a looped line to the next leaf.

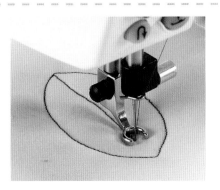

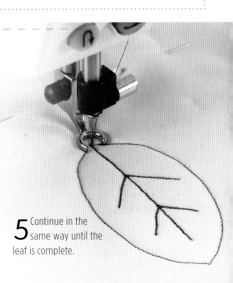

3 Continuing with the same thread, stitch up to the tip of the leaf and, without turning the fabric, stitch back down the vein, right on top of the previous stitches.

4 Stop at the lines that branch off of the main vein and stitch out to the leaf edge and then back on the same line.

5 Continue in the same way until the leaf is complete.

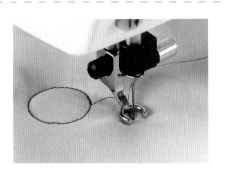

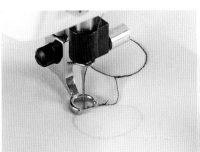

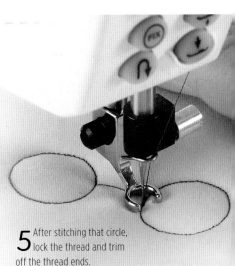

3 Raise the needle and the presser foot. The thread should be loose enough to allow you to slide the fabric to the next area to be stitched.

4 Insert the needle, lock the thread, and continue to stitch, being cautious not to stitch over the jumped thread.

5 After stitching that circle, lock the thread and trim off the thread ends.

Quilting straight lines

Straight line stitching using a walking foot can be both utilitarian and decorative. Straight lines can hold the layers while hiding in the seams of patchwork and borders, or have a graphic impact, adding movement to the open areas of the layout.

When your goal is to form perfect stitches in a straight line, a walking foot attachment or built-in even-feed system will prevent unwelcome shifting of the layers. Both systems work to advance the three individual layers of the quilt bundle from the top in conjunction with the feed dogs, which move the fabric from the bottom. Without these, shifting of the layers causes puckering.

THE WALKING FOOT
The walking foot attachment is an indispensible tool named for the stepping action it makes when the feed dogs are engaged. Stitching is restricted to straight lines or very gentle curves because the quilt bundle must be rotated with every turn. The greatest advantage of using the walking foot is added control.

If your machine did not come with a walking foot, contact a dealer to

Grid marker
This plastic stencil has slots cut in it every ½ in (1.3 cm) and is used to mark parallel lines, squares, and diamonds of varying angles.

purchase one made especially for your machine, or choose a universal walking foot which is manufactured to fit several machines.

THE BUILT-IN EVEN-FEED SYSTEM
Some manufacturers offer machines with an even-feed system. It has a mechanism that works just like the walking foot, and tucks up out of the way when not in use.

Walking foot attachment
This walking foot has a quilting guide attached. The bar is aligned the desired distance from the previous line of stitching to stitch parallel lines without marking.

QUILTING WITH A WALKING FOOT
Try some practice stitching with the walking foot attached to the machine. Mark several 6-in (15-cm) straight lines that are ½ in (1.3 cm) apart on your practice sample. Remember that when using the walking foot the feed dogs are in the up position, working to move the fabric at the same rate as the foot.

1 Install the walking foot, making sure to attach the side bar to the needle bar.

2 Set the stitch length to 0.5 for the locking stitches, then, after the thread has been locked, to your preferred stitch length (between 2.0 and 3.0).

GRID QUILTING

Grid quilting consists of rows of parallel stitched lines that intersect rows of stitched lines, forming squares or diamonds. Accurately draw the grid lines with the aid of the grid marker stencil (see left).

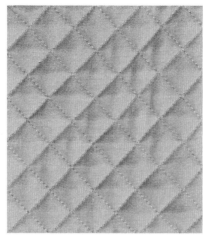

For a checkerboard, draw a grid parallel to the sides of the quilt. Stitch the entire grid and add stippling in every other square.

A grid on point should be planned so that each square or diamond (on point) touches the outline of the space it is filling. Draw lines at the desired angle by aligning the printed lines on the stencil with the outline or seam line that contains the grid.

To mark a basket weave, draw a $1/2$-in (1.3-cm) grid at a 45-degree angle to the sides of the quilt. Draw a rectangle that connects three of the squares, and a second rectangle at a 90-degree angle from the center of the first rectangle. From the center of the second, draw the third, and finally draw a forth rectangle from the center of the third. Stitch each rectangular outline and fill in the empty square formed between the rectangles with stippling.

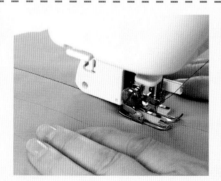

3 Stop stitching just before the end of the line and lock your thread. Trim off top and bobbin thread ends.

4 Quilt the next line, sewing in the same direction and working from the center of the quilt toward the outer edge.

5 Quilt all rows, sewing in the same direction to prevent twisting, and always work from the center outward.

CHANNEL QUILTING

Channel quilting is a versatile technique consisting of simple, straight parallel lines at times equidistant from one another, or set in a patterned repeat. The lines can be used to fill large, empty spaces of the layout, or to fill in around quilted motifs. The straight lines can be blended with circles, stippling, or other designs to create endless pattern possibilities (see right). The lines can either be marked using a quilt marking tool and grid marker stencil, or guided by the use of the walking foot guide bar.

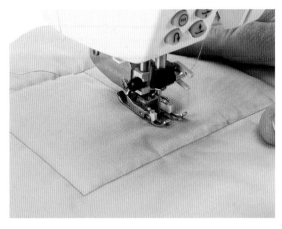

The space that will be filled with the channel lines is first outlined, then divided into sections with lines of stitching.

Multiple lines of channel quilting fill an empty space of the layout with quiet simplicity.

This antique-style pillow by CAROLE SEDGLEY is made from scraps of chintzy fabrics that conjure memories of hot summer days and the smell of flowers. Very close lines using matching thread create an interesting vintage texture to the surface.

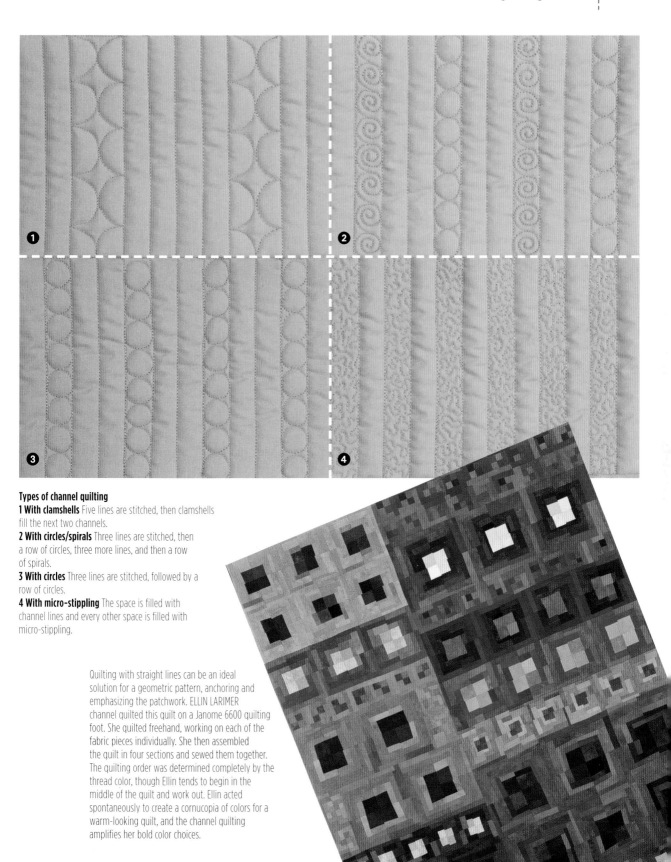

Types of channel quilting
1 With clamshells Five lines are stitched, then clamshells fill the next two channels.
2 With circles/spirals Three lines are stitched, then a row of circles, three more lines, and then a row of spirals.
3 With circles Three lines are stitched, followed by a row of circles.
4 With micro-stippling The space is filled with channel lines and every other space is filled with micro-stippling.

Quilting with straight lines can be an ideal solution for a geometric pattern, anchoring and emphasizing the patchwork. ELLIN LARIMER channel quilted this quilt on a Janome 6600 quilting foot. She quilted freehand, working on each of the fabric pieces individually. She then assembled the quilt in four sections and sewed them together. The quilting order was determined completely by the thread color, though Ellin tends to begin in the middle of the quilt and work out. Ellin acted spontaneously to create a cornucopia of colors for a warm-looking quilt, and the channel quilting amplifies her bold color choices.

An introduction to free-motion quilting

There is incredible freedom when you drop the feed dogs and learn free-motion quilting, but it takes a little practice to feel in control. This information will get you started.

Simple wide zigzags add contrast.

Free-motion spirals give interest to this plain fabric.

Straight lines give a sense of perspective.

When LORIS BOGUE wants curves or curlicues, she chooses free motion. If the quilting needs to fit in a particular space (such as around the blue leaves), she marks the motifs with a chalk pencil and then quilts freehand to fill areas without marking.

Free-motion quilting is a process used for stitching the layers of a quilt together with the feed dogs lowered and a darning foot installed. When the feed dogs are not engaged to advance the fabric, you control the stitch length by the distance you move the quilt before your foot presses the pedal to make another stitch.

As long as the feed dogs can be lowered or covered, free-motion quilting can be performed on any machine, including long- and short-arm quilting machines, or a domestic machine. Much of the information for stitching designs given over the following pages will be valuable regardless of the type of machine you choose to use.

CHOOSE A SPECIFIC FOOT FOR A SPECIFIC TASK

When you free-motion quilt, the foot merely hovers over the layers, gently bouncing as it protects your fingers from the needle. Feet that have been engineered for free-motion quilting vary greatly in design and size. You may need to use more than one during the quilting process depending on the task it will perform, the weight of the thread, and the size of the stitches you intend to make.

Closed darning foot
This closed darning foot is included with many machines. It is fine for practicing the technique, but you may need to use other free-motion feet as your work progresses.

Open-toe free-motion foot
The open-toe free-motion foot was designed for refined free-motion quilting. It is the best foot to use for tiny work because it allows the best view of the needle. This open-toe foot is not suitable for larger quilting because it could catch on longer stitches.

Large free-motion foot
To anchor the layers, or for larger stitches, use a large free-motion foot. This foot is also useful for furrowing deep through thick fabrics or large quilt bundles.

Pin pointer
Remember: the feed dogs must be lowered for free-motion quilting.

Closed object

Multi-object design

Continuous line design

All-over design

DESIGNS FOR FREE-MOTION QUILTING

Some free-motion quilters like to follow a marked line, while others love to draw with the needle. Pattern lines might be precisely planned to the final detail and drawn on the quilt top, or they can simply be imagined as you stitch across the open canvas. Whichever technique you use, all of the quilted designs are formed by a line of stitching that is guided by the quilter moving the quilt.

Design possibilities increase when the stitching is unrestricted; feel free to roam wherever you choose. You can steer in any direction, forming curvilinear or straight lines. The entire quilting process, even straight lines that anchor the seam lines or decorative grids, can be stitched entirely with free-motion quilting.

The designs available for free-motion quilters to stitch fall into several categories:

There are simple **closed objects**, often referred to as motifs. These can be isolated objects that hold the layers with stitching, or a highlighted jewel used with a background filler. Motifs can be arranged to create borders, blocks, and wreaths.

Multi-object designs tend to be a bit more advanced; they may be a group of overlapping objects forming a garland or wreath. These designs usually require retracing and numerous starts and stops.

A continuous line design is line art that represents objects with some sort of tail or line of stitching that leads to the next object. These designs tend to make rows of designs used to fill a narrow space across the quilt top or along a border space.

All-over designs can be anything from simple stippling to elaborate flowers and curls. The scale of a design can dictate whether it is used for a large all-over pattern to fill the entire quilt surface or as a tiny background filler.

Stippling

The most common background fill pattern is stippling. Once you become skilled at the curves and consistent stitching density of this graceful yet minimal filler, you can move on to stitching all sorts of complex patterns with ease.

Stippling, meandering, and micro-stippling are three names given to the same pattern of continuous lines of puzzle shapes and wormlike bodies with lightbulb heads. The difference between the three is the scale of the pattern that is created. Meandering is the largest (the line may be spaced as much as 2–3 in [5–7.5 cm] apart; lines less than 1/2–1/4 in (12–6 mm) apart are referred to as stippling; and smallest of all is micro-stippling.

Stippling is not drawn on the quilt; with practice it is created with a stitching pattern that is imprinted in the brain. It can be used to fill empty spaces around patchwork or appliqué, or to fill in the background after motifs are stitched. If stippling is used in conjunction with a quilted motif, the density of the stippled background should contrast with the volume of the motif.

MICRO-STIPPLING

Intricate motifs surrounded by quiet background space are often filled with micro-stippling, especially in heirloom quilted artwork. You will come to rely on it to flatten the background while calling no attention to itself, establishing a quiet zone that allows the designs to have a strong voice. It gives your eye a place to rest among the activity of all the other images.

Pin pointer
When working on your quilt, visualize the entire blank space that needs to be filled with stippling before you begin. Begin at the bottom edge of a space, the area that is closest to you, and work away from yourself. This will give you the best view of where you have been and where you need to go next.

A note on stitch speed

There is a direct correlation between the speed you are telling the machine to stitch (by pressing the foot pedal), and the distance you move the quilt bundle with your hands. If your pattern is small scale, avoid sharp points in the stitching line by making small stitches; this is done by not moving the bundle very far before you tell the machine to make another stitch. Moving your hands too fast when the machine is running slowly will create long, jagged stitches.

PLANNING AND EXECUTING STIPPLING

The ultimate aim is to stitch stippling shapes without an underdrawing, but in order to do so you need to be able to draw them in the first place. Practice drawing and stitching the shapes to help you plan the pattern evenly and consistently. You will begin to feel the flow of the curving shapes, without points. You need to negotiate around objects and in narrow spaces without crossing lines and leaving rivers of unquilted space.

1 Practice drawing stippling curves on a piece of scrap paper. When you think you have a feel for the curves, use a water-soluble pen to mark a practice bundle.

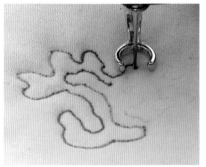

2 Adjust the tension of your machine for your thread. Follow the lines with free-motion quilting. Try moving the fabric toward you as you quilt, to see what you have stitched. Then practice moving the fabric front to back, side to side. Once you become comfortable with the technique, you will begin to develop your own style of stippling.

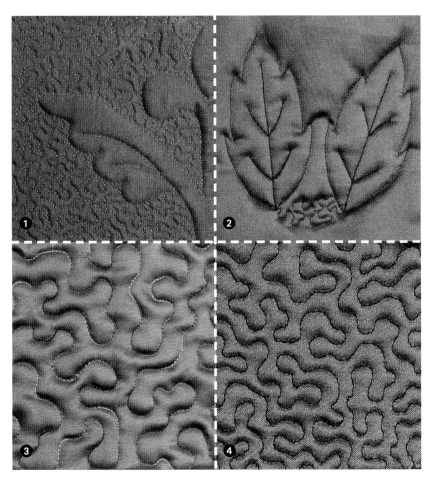

Styles of stippling

1 Micro-stippling as a background filler To create micro-stippling like this, use the smallest free-motion foot available to see where you have been and where you need to stitch next.

2 Traveling from one motif to another When you don't want to use a separate thread, use stippling to travel from one motif to another.

3 Variegated threads Become comfortable with the snaking lines of the pattern with a large-scale meandering project using a medium-weight variegated thread.

4 Stippling in a medium-weight thread Use a tiny thread and don't move the bundle very far to create neat stippling in a medium-weight thread.

3 Now it's time to translate what you've learned on the practice bundle, onto a quilt project. Stitch a wormlike shape with a lightbulb head. Add a line that echoes the worm shape while traveling to the next place to make another stipple shape. The echo lines will give the eye a place to rest. Try not to cross your line of stitching and don't let it bother you if it does happen.

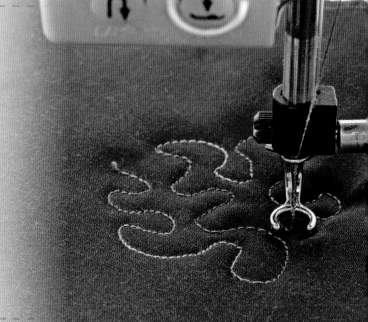

Pin pointer
Maintain a consistent distance between the stitching. Remember, the closer together the rows are the more time they will take to complete, and more thread! As you continue to practice you can refine the size of your stitching, from meandering to stippling to micro-stippling.

Echo quilting

Echo quilting is a simple concept that makes a big impact. Echo lines create an elegant background that allows the motif it surrounds to be the star of the show. Often seen in the hand-quilted masterpiece quilts from the past, you can reproduce a similar look with your machine.

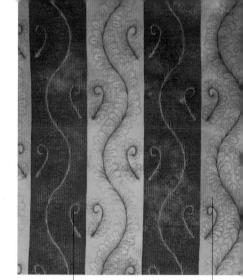

Echo quilting follows the outer edge of other quilting designs, patchwork, or appliqué shapes with stitched lines spaced an equal distance from each other. These lines flatten the surrounding area and allow the featured designs to puff up and catch the light. When numerous rows are used they give the effect of tiny ripples on the surface of a lake.

HOW MANY LINES SHOULD I STITCH?

Stitch as many lines as it takes to fill the background space until you meet another shape, or the echo lines that surround another shape. The lines are not marked on the quilt top, although you may wish to indicate where the lines that surround one design end or bump into the echo lines that surround another motif. Sometimes an interesting secondary pattern is created where the echo lines of two motifs meet.

HOW FAR APART SHOULD THE LINES BE?

The distance between the rows is determined by the scale of the other quilting throughout the piece. A large, round, plastic free-motion foot is often used to echo quilt. The foot has a ring imprinted in the plastic indicating a 1/4 in (6 mm) line, which is used to guide the foot along the outline of the motif or the previous line of stitching. If a wider distance between lines is desired, use the outer edge of the foot as a guide. For lines that are closer together, use a tiny open-toe free-motion foot.

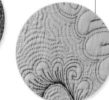

Contrasting threads emphasize the motifs.

Pin pointers

The weight of thread you use should be dependent on the size of stitches desired.

If you want the stitches to blend into the background, use a lightweight thread in a color chosen to match the fabric.

SALLY BRAMALD's quilt was free-motion quilted with only the spines of the feathers being marked as a guide. The small gap between the lobes of each feather was echo quilted once outside the feather, the same distance as this gap. Then the background was echo quilted up to the seams in a thread matching the background.

HOW TO ECHO QUILT

As with any other type of free-motion quilting, learning to echo quilt takes time and practice. Get out your practice bundle, draw a few motifs, and give it a try.

1 First, outline the motif with free-motion ditch quilting (also called outline quilting). Concentrate on stitch length consistency and keep the distance between stitching lines even.

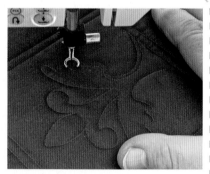

2 When you come to the end of your first round, follow the outline of the motif or the anchoring stitches to get to the place to begin a new line, and guide the edge of the foot to keep the same distance between the lines of stitching.

ECHO QUILTING AROUND A MOTIF

This example shows lines of echo quilting surrounding the Quinn quilting design centered in a square space. The background space is filled with echo quilting that follows both the square frame and the motif outlines, forming interesting patterns where they meet.

BEFORE

AFTER

ECHO QUILTING WITHIN A MOTIF

Here the echo lines are stitched within the feathered heart motif. The lines are not marked on the quilt top; instead, the motif is followed with lines equidistant from one another.

BEFORE

AFTER

Background fillers

Experimenting with free-form and formal background fillers can take you on an adventure of discovery. The design possibilities are unlimited, as the needle of your machine becomes your pencil.

Terms used to describe background filler patterns vary. When describing fills directed by a pattern imprinted on the brain, some people use the term "freehand," while others refer to "free-form" fillers. In this book, "freehand" refers to steering the machine without a marked line, while "free-form" describes the design of a fill pattern that lacks the structure of a marked line. The resulting style is random and less formal. These patterns fill spaces with unstructured, continuous movement and may represent objects such as leaves or

stars, or be completely random lines of loops or meandering.

FREE-FORM FILLERS
With any free-form fill pattern you need to understand how the lines turn and bend before you can steer the sewing machine on a familiar path. Good advice to follow here is: *If you draw it, you can stitch it.*

If you intend to fill your quilt with free-form stitching without marking, you had better take the time to imprint the pattern in your brain. Look closely

at the lines you want to stitch. Trace them with your finger, then draw them on paper. The more senses you involve, the more you will aid the brain in memorizing what you want to imprint. If you do not need to lift your pencil while you are drawing, you can stitch a continuous line.

If a free-form pattern is used to fill a complex space, lay a piece of tracing paper over the quilt top and trace the outline of the space to be filled, then practice drawing the pattern until a stitching path is developed.

Loop-d-loops

Clamshells

Pumpkin seed

Pebbles

Lazy daisy

Checkerboard

Spinning "S"s

Headbands

Lazy daisy

Five teardrop-shaped petals join at a central base to form delicate flowerets.
1 Begin by locking the thread and stitching a $1/2$-in (1.3-cm) teardrop shape forming the first petal.
2 Add a line up the center of the petal.
3 Return to the base and stitch four more petals with lines. Stitch along the edge of a petal to the center base of the next flower. Continue filling the space in this manner. There may be times when fewer petals are needed to fill the space.

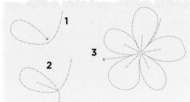

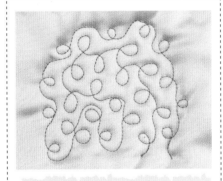

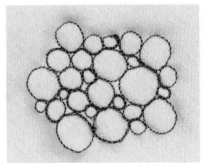

Headbands

One headband consists of a set of rounded arch-shaped lines. There may be as few as two lines in the set, or as many as five. Each set has two bases, one at each end of the arch. It may appear as if the set begins with an upside-down teardrop, because each headband series is spaced in the valley created by two previously stitched headbands.
1 Begin a set by locking the thread and stitching an arch $1/2$ in (1.3 cm) tall.
2 Stitch a second arch in the opposite direction, with $1/8$–$1/4$ in (3–6 mm) of space between the lines at the highest point of the arch, returning to the opposite base.
3 Continue stitching arches until you have returned to the base at the side of the headband where you intend to stitch the second set. You may wish to have identical headbands or alter the orientations of the arches. Try to keep even consistency between the lines and spaces.

Loop-d-loops

This filler looks like a string that has loops connected to one another by a curved line.
1 Begin stitching a lowercase "e."
2 Reverse the direction you make the line to connect to the second "e," which is stitched upside down. Continue filling the space with a snaking line of loops, trying to make your path unrecognizable. For more variety with the pattern, add stars, hearts, or other simple motifs.

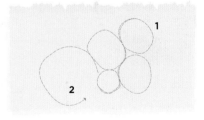

Pebbles

The key to stitching attractive pebbles is to vary the size of the circles.
1 Begin stitching a circular shape. Stitch completely around the circle at least once. It may be necessary to retrace a portion of the first circle in order to travel to where you wish to begin the next pebble.
2 Continue stitching more pebbles, varying the sizes to create large, medium, and small circles that fill in tiny spaces.

Creating your own patterns

Once you have studied and mastered the background fillers offered in this book, you can create your own patterns that express the style of a particular quilt. You will find inspiration for patterns everywhere you go. Keep a camera handy to capture inspiration wherever you are, and use a sketchbook to doodle designs in idle moments.

FORMAL FILLERS

Unlike free-form fillers, formal fillers require a marked foundation of lines, circles, and grids. These examples use the intersections of a marked grid as guides for creating repeating curved designs. Mark the grid using a water-soluble marker and a grid marker stencil, and stitch with feed dogs lowered and a free-motion foot.

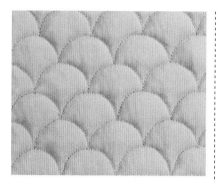

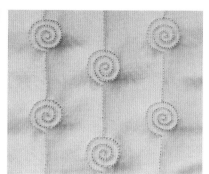

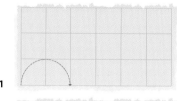

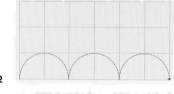

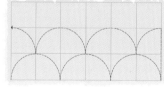

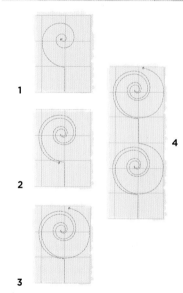

Clamshells

Clamshells are simple arched lines set in staggered rows. Each arch is one grid square high, and two squares wide.

1 Begin at the bottom left corner of the space and curve your line of stitching up to meet the intersection of the next grid line, creating a half-arch, then curve down again to meet the next intersection.

2 Continue stitching arches across the row until you reach the outline.

3 Stitch along the outline to the top of the grid, because the second row of arches will start with a half-arch. Fill the rows, retracing the outline of the space when necessary to get to the next line to be stitched. Details can be added within each arch for added interest.

Lollipops

Lollipops are whimsical patterns made of straight lines with spirals stitched at repeated intervals. When rows of lollipops are used side by side, the rows have alternating spacing for the spirals. Use a grid marker stencil to mark parallel lines and a circle marker template to mark circles, alternating the circle height in every other row.

1 Begin by bringing your thread to the top and locking the stitches at the bottom of the first row. Stitch up the line and stitch the spiral to the center.

2-3 Retrace the spiral back out to the place at the top where the line continues up to the next spiral.

4 Continue stitching the rows of lollipops to fill the area.

1   **2**

3

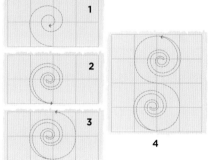

1

2

3

4

Pin pointers

Threads for background fillers will vary according to the look you desire. They can range from medium-weight colorful variegated to bold and glitzy metallic to the finest lightweight silk that matches the color of the fabric. Heavyweight thread is not a good choice for small-scale patterns because the dense stitches not only look unattractive, but it is difficult to negotiate tight curves with a large needle and thick thread.

The scale of the pattern determines where it can be used. The same tiny pattern used to fill in around stitched motifs can easily be expanded to cover your whole quilt top with a large-scale all-over pattern stitched from edge to edge.

Pumpkin seed

This pattern is based on a grid that is marked but not stitched. You will use the grid intersections only as a guide for creating repeated curved lines.

1 Mark a grid at a 45-degree angle to the edge of the quilt. Lock the threads near the middle of the bottom row. Stitch shallow curved lines all the way to the top of the line, pivot, then snake your way to the next space outline.

2 Continue until you meet the starting place, then stitch the "S" curve on the opposite side of the line. When you complete the first round, stitch along the outline of the space to get to the next available line. Remember to turn the piece if it is easier to stitch consistent curves.

3 Fill all of the lines in this manner to complete the pattern.

Spinning "S"s

This is essentially a continual stack of spirals. The movement of your hands when directing this design is just like writing a stack of the letter "S," one on top of another. Two different effects are achieved by stitching the grid lines and adding a spiral in each square, or marking the grid without stitching as a placement guide for each spiral.

1 Mark a grid that is parallel to the edge of the quilt. Lock your thread along the outline at the bottom of the grid. Stitch a small spiral in the center of the first grid square.

2 Retrace that line back out until you kiss the bottom of the square.

3 Echo the shape back up.

4 Continue the stack of spirals in the squares above. You can rotate the fabric and retrace the outline to get to a new row of spirals, or lock your thread and begin at the bottom if the shape is more consistent when stitched in the same direction.

Trapunto

There are times when machine quilters would like to accentuate specific motifs within the quilt layout. This technique, called "trapunto," adds additional fullness to motifs, or any area of a design you may want to puff out.

Pin pointer
Consider the distortion that can occur when adding an extra layer of batting only to some areas of the layout. If designs are filled too full, they bulge out, causing the edges of the quilt to ripple.

In Italian the word *trapunto* means "to embroider," and in Latin it means "to prick with a needle." This technique was traditionally done by hand stitching a motif's outline that was later stuffed with extra batting from the back of the quilt. A modern-day version of the process was invented by machine quilter Hari Walner.

BATTING FOR TRAPUNTO
Batting for machine trapunto is a matter of choice. Often the two layers are not of the same fiber content. If an 80/20 cotton blend is to be the main batting, either wool or polyester could be used for added loft while still remaining soft. If a very hard fullness is desired, a cotton batting could be used for both layers.

THREAD FOR TRAPUNTO
The invention of water-soluble thread was a real bonus for machine trapunto. It is manufactured from a corn base that dissolves completely in water. Originally the technique called for threading the machine with the water-soluble thread in the needle and lightweight thread in the bobbin. This method trapped the bobbin thread in the layers after the top thread washed away. You may choose to use the water-soluble in both top and bobbin. Or, to save on the expense if there is a lot of trapunto planned, use the lightweight in the top and the water-soluble in the bobbin, then the top thread will be released and fall away when the water-soluble bobbin thread dissolves.

MACHINE TRAPUNTO
The technique for trapunto by machine follows a similar plan to that used for free-motion quilting a top, but adds one extra step.

1 Prepare the top by stabilizing, pressing, and marking all designs.

2 Baste a layer of batting only (without the backing fabric) to the areas that are to be accentuated. Secure the two layers together with pins.

Daisy and curly fill patterns make the trapunto motif stand out.

This quilt by JOANIE ZEIER POOLE uses one elegant but simple motif, arranged in a square layout. The double outline of the motif made it perfect for accentuating with trapunto. The background was flattened with daisy and curly fill patterns using decorative thread, allowing the extra fullness of the motif to pop.

3 Thread the machine with water-soluble thread in the needle and lightweight thread in the bobbin. Stitch around the outlines of the area to be accentuated.

4 When the stitching is complete, flip the piece to the back side. Trim away the excess batting just outside the stitching line with small scissors. Be careful not to cut the fabric.

5 Finally, the top is layered just as you would for quilting without trapunto. A complete layer of batting and backing fabric is pin-basted and then the entire quilting process is followed using your desired thread.

Finishing

We are at the final leg of the journey; putting the finishing touches on your masterpiece. It's time to launder, bind, and label your quilt with information to identify it.

When you have finished quilting your projects there are a few procedures you need to carry out to make them complete. Honor the many hours of work you have put into the project by using your best skills and highest standards for completing your work. When these last finishing tasks are complete, you can revel in the satisfaction of the final glory of the finished project.

LAUNDERING

First you need to remove the markings, spray starch, and any dirt or dust that may have settled on the project while in progress. The procedure for this job will depend on the size of the project and your laundry facilities. If it is small, you can use almost any sink or a plastic tub. If your piece is large, place it in a plastic laundry basket in a bath tub.

Don't be afraid to get your quilt wet. When the piece is wet it becomes submissive and can be persuaded into the flat and accurate shape required.

Submerge the entire piece in cold water only. For quilts that have been heavily marked, this cold water rinse may need to be repeated if, when dry, the marks reappear. Use cold water only until you are sure the water-soluble marking is completely gone. Then it is safe to use a gentle quilt soap. Allow most of the water to drain away, then lift the quilt out in the basket.

DRYING

Next, roll the quilt up in beach towels to absorb most of the water. Never wring the quilted piece, rather blot it with absorbent towels to remove excess water. Lay the quilt out flat to dry on a waterproof surface or the floor. If necessary, gently persuade the quilt into shape with your hands, patting it down as required. An electric fan can be used to speed the drying time.

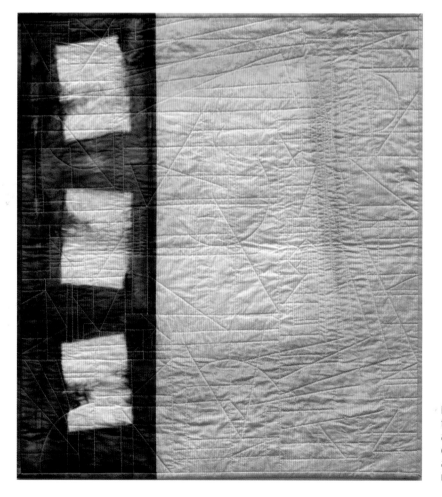

Matching the binding fabric to the quilt, even changing the binding fabric partway along one side, makes it almost invisible. For JEANETTE MEYER, choosing a two-colored binding was an integral part of the design, allowing the composition to be subtly framed while remaining bifurcated.

SQUARING UP THE QUILT

When the quilt is dry it is completely stable. Unless you get it wet again, it will no longer shrink, pucker, or stretch, so this is the perfect time to square the piece up and add the binding. You will need a rotary cutter, self-healing cutting mat, and long plastic ruler. If the quilt is small enough, slide the mat under it and align the quilt edge with the lines on the mat, then trim all four sides evenly. Use the lines of the mat to keep the quilt square.

If the quilt is large, keep it on the floor and slide one or more large cutting mats under it. Use a long carpenter's straight edge to keep lines straight. Align the ruler an equal distance from one feature of the quilt, and trim away excess fabric and batting from all four sides. Now you have a perfectly straight, neat edge with which to align the binding.

FINISHING

The outer edge of a quilt can be finished in many different ways; bringing the backing to the front, folding both the top and backing in to meet one another in a knife edge, or by adding additional fabric strips to cover the raw edges. The most durable finish is the double fold bias binding (see pages 94–95).

The last detail to add to your quilt is a label. Labels can be embroidered, printed from a computer, or made with scraps left over from the quilt. Sew the label to the back of your project to record information about the quilter, the dimensions, occasion, and the date the quilt was completed.

Quiltmaker MARIJKE DE BOER-BOON has a large (40 x 40 in/100 x 100 cm) cutting mat for truing up the quilt layers, which she uses on the floor. She uses a Photoshop program for designing labels printed with her name and address. These are printed onto transfer paper, reversed, and ironed onto fabric. Bindings are double-ironed strips 2¼ in (5.7 cm) wide.

PREPARING THE BINDING STRIPS

Double fold bias binding strips are cut on a true bias, at a 45-degree angle. They are cut 2¼ in (5.7 cm) wide and folded in half to make a double thickness of sturdy binding. This binding is strong, full-bodied, does not pucker, and wears better than straight-cut strips. It is the best choice to complete the edge of your machine quilted projects, and the only choice if the quilt has curved edges. Strips may be wider if a bolder binding is preferred.

1 Cut a triangle off the corner of your binding fabric on the 45-degree angle line.

2 Rotate the fabric to align the newly cut bias edge with a line on the mat and cut in 2¼ in (5.7 cm) strips. Cut enough strips to make the length needed for the project when joined.

3 Use a ¼ in (6 mm) seam allowance to sew the binding strips together.

4 Pressing the seams open will evenly distribute the layers of fabric, allowing the binding to lie flat.

5 Fold the strip in half lengthwise, with the right side out, and press.

ATTACHING THE BINDING

There are many ways to trim the edge of the quilt with binding. These instructions are for a quilt with a straight edge and square corners. This binding has neat mitered corners and is finished by hand stitching to the back of the quilt. Use a walking foot and a ¼ in (6 mm) seam allowance. For advice on binding a curved edge, see Step 6, page 101.

1 Fold the raw edge of the binding strip under by ¼ in (6 mm).

2 Align the strip with the front of the quilt, matching all raw edges. Starting at the center of the first side, use a walking foot to sew ¼ in (6 mm) from the raw edge. Stop stitching ¼ in (6 mm) from the first corner, backstitch, lift the needle, and clip the threads.

3 To form the mitered corner, fold the binding upward at a 45-degree angle, then back down at 90 degrees over itself, matching the raw edges of the second side.

4 Begin the stitching of each remaining side at the top edge, but stopping ¼ in (6 mm) before the corner. When you return to the first side, overlap the strips, stitch just past the beginning stitches, and backstitch.

5 Finish the binding by turning the folded edge over the quilt edge evenly. Pins or hair clips can hold it in place while you hand sew. Use a neat slipstitch to secure the edge of the binding to the back of quilt. Catch the mitered corners with a few stitches, the quilt judges always look!

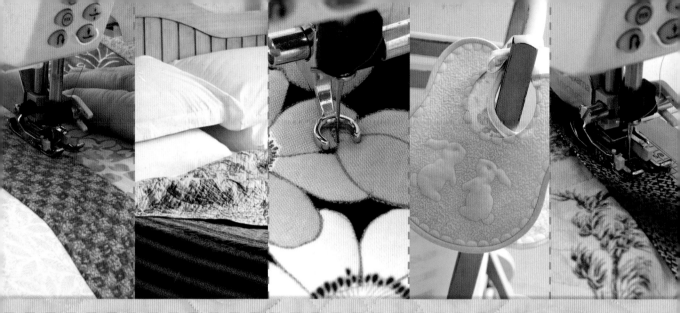

CHAPTER 4
Projects

Now you are ready to sit down at the machine and put all you have learned to good use. Four projects—a sewing caddy, a cute baby bib, and two quilts—have been designed for you with easy-to-follow step-by-step directions. From simple quilt-as-you-go techniques to elegant heirloom machine quilting, each project demonstrates a different quilting technique that will allow you to experience different material choices, quilting styles, and finishing details.

Project 1:
Sewing tool caddy

Construct this sewing tool caddy using the simple quilt-as-you-go technique. Quilt the focus fabric square and coordinating fabric strips as you assemble the caddy front, add the pocket and the binding, and you will be ready to tote your sewing tools to class. You'll find the quilting guide for this project on page 125.

YOU WILL NEED

- 5½-in (14-cm) square of focus fabric
- ½ yd (0.5 m) fabric for backing and binding
- ½ yd (0.5 m) fabric for the pocket
- ¼ yd (0.2 m) scraps of coordinating cotton fabrics
- ⅓ yd (0.3 m) firm batting, 80/20 cotton/polyester
- Thread for piecing
- 1½-in (3.8-cm) piece of hook-and-loop closure tape
- Three-ring zippered pouch and 21 in (53 cm) of ½ in (1.2 cm) wide ribbon (for ties)
- 40 wt/3-ply trilobal polyester for decorative quilting (optional)
- Spray baste (optional)
- Washable white school glue (optional)

ABOUT THE TECHNIQUE USED

Quilt-as-you-go is one term used for two different machine quilting techniques. With the first technique a quilt top is assembled, layered, and quilted in separate sections that are sewn together to make the larger quilt. However, since in this book we work by handling large quilts as one piece, this project will teach you the other quilt-as-you-go technique: quilting the layers as you assemble the patchwork. Begin by cutting the backing fabric and batting to the size of the finished caddy. These full-size layers create a foundation on which you will build the patchwork layout, quilting the layers as you sew the seams. The caddy pattern uses a square of focus fabric to which fabric strips are stitched in sequential order until the entire caddy cover is complete. This quilt-as-you-go technique works well for small projects, up to crib-size quilts.

CUTTING PLAN

Base fabric
24 x 12 in (61 x 30.5 cm)

Focus fabric
5½ x 5½ in (14 x 14 cm)

Flap
3½ x 10 in (9 x 25 cm)

Pocket
23 x 13 in (58 x 33 cm)

A strips
Four 1½ x 5½ in (3.8 x 14 cm), each from a different coordinating fabric

B strips
Four 1½ x 9½ in (3.8 x 24 cm), each from a different coordinating fabric

C strips
Five 2½ x 10 in (6.4 x 25 cm), each from a different coordinating fabric

Binding
Cut enough 2¼ in (5.7 cm) bias strips to make a 72-in (183-cm) assembled strip

Batting
23 x 11 in (58 x 28 cm)

PROJECT DIMENSIONS

The finished caddy is 9½ x 10 in (24 x 25.5 cm) when closed and 22 x 10 in (56 x 25.5 cm) when open. The cut sizes may be adjusted to the size of the motif used in your focus fabric, or the entire size of the caddy can be adjusted to the size of your specific tools.

Pin pointer
Remember to stabilize fabrics with spray starch for accurate cutting.

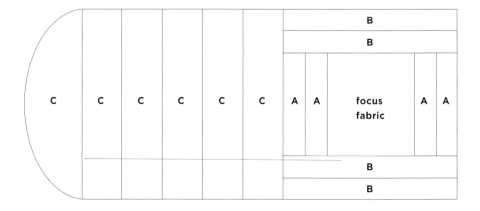

ASSEMBLING

1 Lay the backing fabric, wrong side up. Center the batting on the backing. Most batting will stick to the base without shifting—if not, use basting spray or straight pins to hold the layers as you stitch. Place the focus fabric 3 in (7.5 cm) from the left end and 2½ in (6.4 cm) from the top and bottom edges of the backing. Be sure that it is aligned accurately as all of the seams will be based on this placement. Use a pin or two to hold the position securely.

2 Place one A-strip at the right edge of the focus square, right sides together, aligning the raw edges. Use two pins to hold it in place. Install the walking foot and use a ¼-in (6-mm) seam allowance to sew the seam. Use the machine locking stitch feature, or backstitch each end of the seam to hold it securely. Make sure the seam looks good on the back because the stitching will be seen on the inside of the caddy.

3 Flip the fabric back so that the right side is facing up and finger press the seam open. Some stiff fabrics may need to be pressed with an iron.

4 Align a second A-strip on the first one, with right sides facing. Accurately align, pin, sew the seam, and press open. Place pins to hold the piece in place.

5 Repeat the same process, sewing the two remaining A-strips to the opposite side of the focus square, press the seams, and pin the edge.

6 Add the four B-strips to the sides of the center panel in the same manner.

7 When the front half of the caddy is complete, add the five C-strips, using the same technique. Be sure that the first piece is aligned accurately at a 90-degree angle and that it covers the ends of the strips.

8 The wider flap strip is the final strip to sew. After the flap has been attached, flipped, and pressed, sew a row of stitching around the entire piece, $^3/_{16}$ in (4.7 mm) from the edge and remove all pins.

9 Quilt the flap, focus square, or any of the other fabrics if desired. Use a decorative thread or any quilting thread and a lightweight bobbin thread, remembering that the stitching will show on the inside of the caddy.

FINISHING

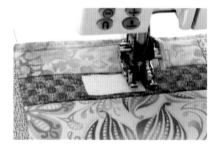

1 Sew the loop piece of a strip of hook-and-loop closure tape to the center of the first A-strip piece.

2 To make the lined pocket, fold the pocket fabric in half lengthwise to $6^1/_2$ x 23 in (16.5 x 58 cm) and press. With the caddy inside facing up and the front flap on the left side, align the raw edges of the pocket with the caddy edges. Pin the pocket and sew $^3/_{16}$ in (4.7 mm) in from the sides and bottom edges.

3 Trim the outside edge of the caddy using the pattern on page 125 to cut the flap shape and trimming along the ends of the strips.

Simple quilting enhances the quilted motif.

4 Sew the lines that will be the sections of the pockets to hold the tools. Divide those sections by measuring your tools and making a plan to stitch the sections according to your needs. The stitching will look best if you flip the caddy to the front side and stitch in the ditch of the strip seams, so place a pin in the back and then stitch the closest seam from the front.

5 Sew the hook piece of the hook-and-loop closure tape to the center of the inside of the flap. Hand stitches can be hidden in the layers; machine stitching will show on the front.

6 Cut 2¼ in (5.7 cm) of bias binding, assemble the strips, and press in half lengthwise according to the instructions on page 94. Attach the binding to the front of the caddy, with the overlapped ends on the bottom of the caddy on the center fold. Two of the corners will be mitered and two of the corners will be rounded with the binding strip eased along the curved edge. Fold the binding to the inside. If desired, use a tiny line of washable white school glue to hold the edge in place, and heat-set the glue to dry with a dry iron.

7 Hand stitch the binding edge from the back (or work from the front and use a decorative machine stitch with decorative thread, as shown here) to stitch over the ditch, around the entire binding seam.

8 To attach a three-ring zippered pouch, sew three 7-in (17.8-cm) pieces of ribbon on the center seam and tie a knot at each hole.

Now that your caddy is complete, fill it with quilting tools.

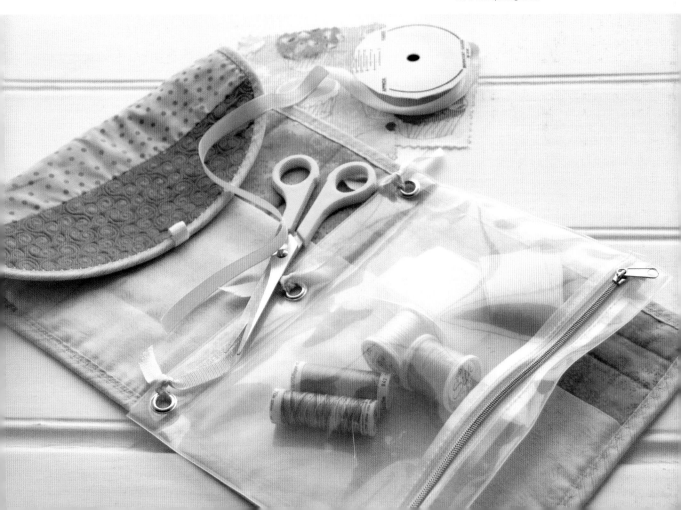

Project 2:
Polka-dot quilt

This polka-dot quilt uses an inventive assembly process, creating the quilt top for the fun of quilting in a flash. You will apply one central piece of fabric over a one-piece background and cover the raw edge with rickrack, eliminating the need for piecing or mitering the border corners. After the rickrack is attached, simply flip the quilt top over and trim away the extra layer of fabric and your top is ready to layer for quilting.

CUTTING PLAN

Center fabric
22 x 36 in (56 x 91 cm)

Faux border
42 x 54 in (1.07 x 1.37 m)

Backing fabric
44 x 54 in (1.11 x 1.37 m)

Bias binding strips
Enough 2¼-in (5.7-cm) binding to make a total of 210 in (5.3 m) when assembled

YOU WILL NEED

- ⅔ yd (0.6 m) polka-dot fabric for top center
- 1½ yd (1.5 m) daisy-print fabric for faux borders
- ½ yd (0.5 m) coordinating fabric for binding
- 1½ yd (1.5 m) coordinating fabric for backing
- 1½ yd (1.5 m) batting, preferrably wool
- 4 yd (4 m) of wide rickrack
- Invisible or 50/60 wt/2-ply thread to match outlines of border fabric
- 40 wt/3-ply trilobal polyester variegated thread for meandering
- Washable white school glue

PROJECT DIMENSIONS
Finished size is 40 x 52 in (1.02 x 1.32 m).

Pin pointers
Remember, all fabrics should be prewashed and stabilized with spray starch.

Take care when cutting fabric with printed motifs to align them with the ruler. Some fabrics may need to be gently persuaded into a perfect rectangle with spray starch and an iron.

ABOUT THE TECHNIQUE USED
This project offers you a chance to practice two simple free-motion skills; stitching large-scale meanderings over the polka dots, and following the outline of the flowers and leaves on the faux border. The binding has mitered corners and is finished with a decorative machine-stitched edge. With no seams to sew, and no marking, this is a quick and easy project.

This quilt features a polka-dot fabric for the center and a sassy, large-scale daisy print for the faux borders. Faux rickrack was cut from a coordinating fabric to get the exact size needed to fit between each polka dot. To do this, draw the rickrack on paper-backed fusible web then fuse to the fabric. Cut out the rickrack and fuse this to the quilt top, covering the edge of the polka-dot fabric. Manufactured rickrack can be used rather than making your own.

The rickrack was handmade in the finished project, to give a more organic look.

ASSEMBLING

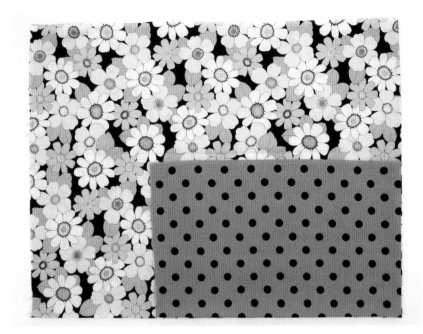

1 Work on a large pressing surface. Press the prewashed and stabilized faux border fabric in half in both directions, creasing lines that will be used to align the center fabric. Press the center rectangle fabric in half in both directions. Place the center rectangle fabric on the faux border fabric, aligning the creases.

2 Beginning at any corner, cover the edge of the center fabric with rickrack. Plan to turn the corners with a point of the rickrack pointing toward the outside corner of the quilt. Hold the corner with a pin.

3 Place a tiny line of glue along both edges of the rickrack to adhere both fabrics. Leave the beginning end free to join the final end after all sides are attached, and use a ruler to check it is aligned with the outside edge of the quilt. Heat-set the glue with a dry iron. When the end from the fourth side meets the beginning end, create the corner point and overlap slightly. The raw edges of the end, as well as both of the outside edges of the rickrack, can either be stitched now or during the quilting process.

4 Turn the quilt top to the back and carefully make a slit in the fabric to slide scissors in between the two fabric layers and trim away the unnecessary faux border layer from behind the polka-dot center.

QUILTING

1 Baste the layers using your preferred method (see pages 60–62). You may use either the free-motion foot or the walking foot to anchor the layers. Use thread to match the rickrack. Set the needle down feature if you have it.

2 Begin quilting by anchoring the layers with lines of stitching that will secure the layers and allow you to remove some of the pins. Remember to lock your thread at the beginning and end of every line of stitching. Secure the rickrack by stitching a line on the rickrack, along both edges. Stitch around the entire outer edge of the top, $^3/_{16}$ in (4.7 mm) in from the edge.

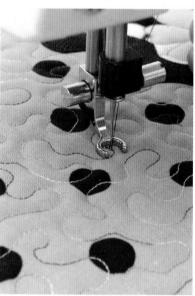

3 The center fabric is quilted with variegated thread in a medium scale meandering pattern. Set up the machine for free-motion quilting and read the meandering suggestions on pages 82–83. Since the space to fill is large, subdivide it into quarter sections. Begin by locking the thread along the rickrack in the middle of any side. Meander a path across the quilt until you meet the rickrack on the other side. Try to stitch a wide enough path that will be difficult to detect when all of the meandering surrounds it. Subdivide the other half of the quilt in the same manner, filling the quadrants with evenly spaced meandering.

4 The final area to quilt is the faux border, using a line of free-motion quilting to outline the daisies. Install a lightweight thread in a color that matches the outline, or use invisible thread. Lock your thread along the rickrack, anywhere on the top. Work along the rickrack, moving toward the outer edge of the quilt. If you get to a dead-end, simply lock your stitches, clip the thread and move to the desired area, lock your threads, and continue stitching until the area is filled.

FINISHING

1 Thoroughly rinse the project to remove the spray starch and lay flat to dry. Lay the project on a large cutting mat and square it up by aligning a ruler the same distance away from the rickrack on each side and trimming away excess layers, providing a perfect edge for adding the binding.

2 Cut enough $2^1/_4$-in (5.7-cm) bias binding strips to make 200 in (5.08 m) when joined. Sew the binding strips together and follow the instructions for double-fold bias binding on page 94.

3 Begin on the bottom edge of the quilt. Use a walking foot for your machine to sew $^1/_4$ in (6 mm) from the raw edge, backstitching at the beginning and end. Finish the binding by turning it over the edge to the back of the quilt. Apply glue and heat-set with a dry iron.

4 Choose a decorative stitch or zigzag stitch to sew the binding. Working from the front of the quilt, align the stitching to catch both the binding edge and the quilt top.

This simple layout utilizes two large rectangles of fabric for a really quick assembly process for the top and a coordinating print to hide the stitching on the back.

Project 3:
Toile bed quilt

This single-bed size quilt is reminiscent of an antique French quilt, which often used large pieces of print fabrics to make a wholecloth style quilt. You will find the quilting guide for this project on page 125.

YOU WILL NEED

- 5 yd (5 m) toile for top front
- 4½ yd (4.5 m) striped fabric for back and binding
- 2 yd (2 m) fabric printed with small motifs in rows for center back
- White marker or color best seen on border fabric
- Single-bed size 100% cotton batting, at least 67 x 89 in (170 x 226 cm)
- 50 wt cotton thread for assembly and quilting

PROJECT DIMENSIONS

The quilt will fit a single bed, 39 x 72 in (99 x 183 cm). A dust ruffle is used on the bed, so the quilt needs to drop 11 in (28 cm) on both sides and at the foot, but not under the pillows. The finished size therefore needs to be 61 x 83 in (155 x 211 cm), plus 7 in (18 cm) added for shrinkage and extra fabric to hold on to while quilting, making the cutting size 68 x 90 in (173 x 229 cm). To make a quilt for a different size of bed, measure the width and length of the mattress and the depth to determine the length of the drop. Then add 8 in (20 cm) to each measurement to determine the cutting size.

This diagram shows the quilting lines that hold the layers of the quilt together. If a fabric printed with motifs repeated in alternating rows is used for the center, you will not need to mark the grid. After assembling the top, mark the border leaf and swags using the pattern on page 125, baste the layers, then simply quilt the center section by stitching the grid lines between the motifs.

ABOUT THE TECHNIQUE USED

This reversible quilt uses a large-scale toile fabric on one side and a paisley fabric center surrounded by a reproduction stripe pieced together for the reverse side. It was quilted with the pieced side up to expose the seam lines for anchoring, and the alternating rows of printed paisleys provide a grid to follow without having to mark the lines. The swag quilting design often seen on vintage quilts, was marked on the back and provides the perfect scalloped pattern for the serpentine binding.

To recreate the puckered layers that give this project a vintage feel, choose 100% cotton batting, which shrinks significantly, and do not prewash the fabrics. After assembling and quilting the layers, wash the quilt in hot water and dry in a dryer.

CUTTING PLAN

Top front fabric
Two 90-in (2.3-m) panels

Center back fabric
60 x 40 in (150 x 100 cm)

Top and bottom back panels
Two 40 x 15-in (100 x 38-cm) strips

Sides of back fabric
Two 15 x 90-in (38 x 230-cm) strips

Bias binding
2¼ in (5.7 cm) wide; 360 in (9.1 m) long

Batting
67 x 89 in (170 x 226 cm)

ASSEMBLING

1 To make the toile side, sew the two panels together, carefully matching the pattern. Use a $^1\!/_2$-in (1.3-cm) seam allowance and press the seams open. Trim to 68 x 90 in (173 x 229 cm) for a single size quilt.

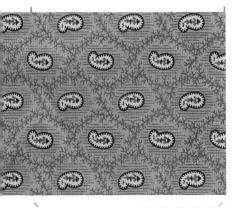

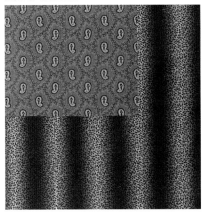
FRONT OF QUILT BACK

BACK OF QUILT BACK

2 To construct the quilt back, sew one striped piece to the top and bottom edges of the toile then sew one long panel to each side. Use a $^1\!/_2$-in (1.3-cm) seam allowance and press the seams open. Make sure the position of the stripe on each side of the toile is identical, so that the stripes match and look like one piece of fabric when sewn on the side panels.

Pin pointer
When cutting a print that will be followed for grid stitching, make sure that the grid points hit the seams. Use a ½ in (1.3 cm) seam allowance for sturdy long seams.

MARKING

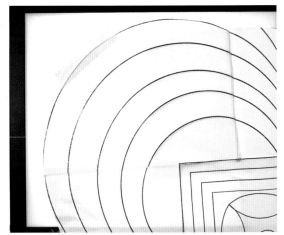

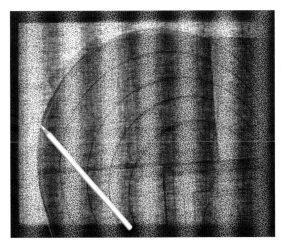

1 Enlarge the quilting design guide on page 125 in three steps using a copy machine. Copy the design and enlarge it 200%. Use that print-out to enlarge by 200% again and once more at 200% for a single size quilt. You only need a section of the leaf and swag borders and one corner. Ask for assistance at the copy center and tape the paper together if necessary.

2 Since the quilt is reversible it can be marked and stitched from either the top or bottom, whichever fabric shows up the marked line best. With the aid of a light box if necessary, use a long ruler to mark the grid on the center fabric, with the grid intersections touching the seams. Next mark the lines, leaves, and swag borders. Baste the layers using your preferred method (see pages 60–62).

QUILTING

1 Using the walking foot, begin quilting by anchoring the top along the straight lines, the seam of the toile panel, the line that is 6 in (15 cm) out from the toile seam, and along the outer edge of the quilt. Next, stitch the grid in the quilt center. Begin by stitching an X over the space to subdivide it into work zones, then continue stitching the grid, rotating the quilt in the same direction each time your stitching meets the boundary of the panel. With the paisley print used here, stitching every other row of motifs yields a 2 in (5 cm) grid. Stitch the straight lines surrounding the leaf border.

2 Using the free-motion foot with the feed dogs lowered, first stitch the continuous line leaf pattern, then the swag pattern that fills the outer edge of the quilt. Work away from the center of the quilt just in case there is any shifting of layers—the excess fabric would be pushed toward the outer edge.

FINISHING

1 When the quilting is complete, before the binding is attached, remove the markings and spray starch by placing the quilt in a sink and letting cold water run through it. To shrink it for the antique puckered look, put the quilt in the washing machine using hot water and a gentle cycle, then dry in a hot dryer.

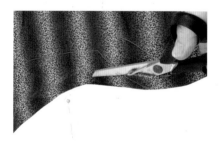

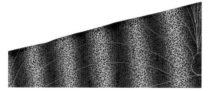

3 Install the walking foot to attach the binding, matching raw edges (see pages 94–95). The serpentine edge is easier to stitch than true scalloped binding, which comes to sharp points between swags. The shallow serpentine curves allow for continuous stitching without fussy inside corners.

4 Turn the binding to the back of the quilt and stitch by hand so the quilt looks pretty with either side facing up.

2 Lay the dry quilt on a large cutting surface to trim the outer edge. Using the enlarged quilting pattern as your guide, follow the serpentine pattern to cut a shallow inward curve ³/₄ in (1.9 cm) away from the stitched outward curve of the swag.

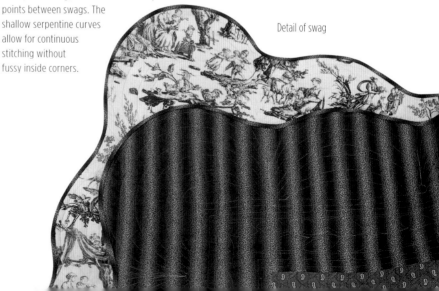

Detail of swag

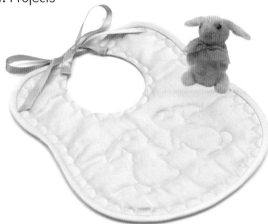

Project 4:
Keepsake baby bib

This adorable baby bib uses elegant fabric and silk thread to create a keepsake for a very special new arrival. Stitch the sweet bunny design, add the binding, and, quick as a wink, you will be ready for the "ohh"s and "ahh"s at the baby shower! Turn to page 124 for the quilting guide.

CUTTING PLAN

Top/backing fabric
12 x 12 in (30 x 30 cm)—to allow extra fabric to hold onto while quilting

Batting
11 x 11 in (28 x 28 cm)—to avoid the inconvenience of having the batting poking out while you work

Single-fold bias strips
Enough 1¼-in (3.2-cm) strips to total 35 in (89 cm) of assembled binding for the bib with a turned neck opening. Or, if you choose to bind the neck opening and use binding to tie the bib, you will need 60 in (152 cm) in total

YOU WILL NEED

- ½ yd (0.5 m) fabric for front and binding
- 12 x 12 in (30 x 30 cm) fabric for backing, coordinating print or juvenile print
- 100 wt silk thread (one small spool)
- 11 x 11 in (28 x 28 cm) wool batting
- 1 yd (1 m) of ½ in (1.3 cm) to 1½ in (3.8 cm) wide ribbon for a tie closure
- Water-soluble marker
- Masking tape

PROJECT DIMENSIONS
Finished size is 8 x 9½ in (20 x 24 cm).

ABOUT THE TECHNIQUE USED

This project may look difficult, but don't be fooled; you will use the refined free-motion skills you learned, choose a special fabric, and follow the bunny outlines with silk thread. Choose a solid color cotton batiste, sateen, or Radiance silk/cotton blend fabric for a keepsake bib—or any pretty cotton for an everyday bib. You can fill the background with a fill pattern or leave the background plain. Two alternatives for finishing the neckline can be tried, binding and adding ribbon ties, or using extra binding as the ties.

Pin pointer
Prewash the top and backing fabric, making sure you use the proper heat setting for the fiber content of any specialty fabric. Stabilize them with a generous application of spray starch to avoid the stretching of layers during cutting, marking, and quilting.

PREPARING

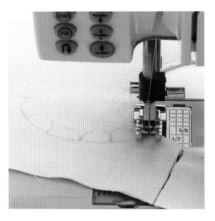

1 Enlarge the template on page 124. The bib was designed to fit a newborn, so you may need to adjust the size of the pattern to the size of the baby. Tape the paper pattern to the work surface. Crease the top fabric in half in each direction as a guide for centering it over the pattern, matching the fold lines. With the fabric positioned over the pattern, tape the edges to avoid shifting. Use a water-soluble marker to trace the design.

2 First you will stitch the neck opening with right sides together. If you cannot see the stitching line easily through the fabric, trace it on the back as well. Place the bib front on top of the backing fabric with right sides facing. Use a short stitch length to stitch the neck opening.

3 Trim the seam to a $^{3}/_{16}$-in (4.7-mm) seam allowance and carefully clip toward the seam at each scallop, taking care not to snip the stitching.

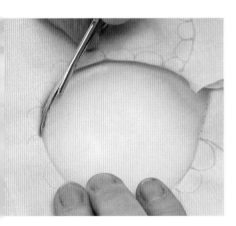

4 Turn the bib right side out and finger-press the neck opening, persuading it to lay flat. Lay the bib on top of the batting and trim away a circle of batting at the neck opening.

5 Slide the batting in between the front and back layers. The batting should be on top of the clipped seam allowance around the neck opening.

6 Use masking tape to tape the backing to the work surface, making sure it is smooth and flat. Smooth the bib front and tape the edges to the work surface. Place a few straight pins to hold the layers, but avoid placing the pins on the stitching lines. Carefully remove the tape.

QUILTING

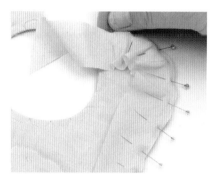

1 Install the free-motion foot and drop the feed dogs. Practice stitching to achieve proper tension with the silk thread. Begin the quilting process by bringing the thread to the top and locking it on the outline at the top of the bib. Stitch around the entire outline of the neck opening, including the scallops, and lock the thread.

2 Begin a new thread by locking the stitches on the outline of the bunny tail. Stitch the circular shape of the tail, then stitch the entire bunny outline, locking the thread just past the place where you began stitching. Lock the thread and stitch the eye. Repeat for the other bunny. Fill the background around the bunnies with micro-stippling or any other fill pattern, if desired.

3 The outer edge of the bib is finished with a 35-in (89-cm) strip of single-fold bias binding. (It differs from double-fold binding in that it is cut 1¼ in (3.2 cm) and sewn on as a single layer, without folding in half lengthwise.) Find the center of the strip and match it to the center on the bottom edge of the bib front. Align the raw edges and pin the binding to the bib front.

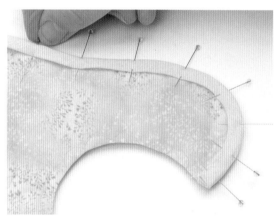

5 Turn the binding to the back, folding the raw edge under. The binding should be ⅜ in (1 cm) wide on the back. Tuck the raw edges in at the end of the opening: this will be covered by the ribbon. Pin to secure while stitching.

4 Use a walking foot or regular sewing foot and a ¼-in (6-mm) seam allowance to attach the binding.

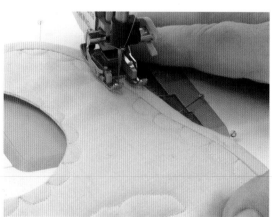

6 Turn the bib to the front side and stitch in the ditch of the seam, catching the folded edge on the back. Rinse the bib with cold water and lay it flat to dry. Attach 15 in (38 cm) of manufactured ribbon to each side of the neck opening.

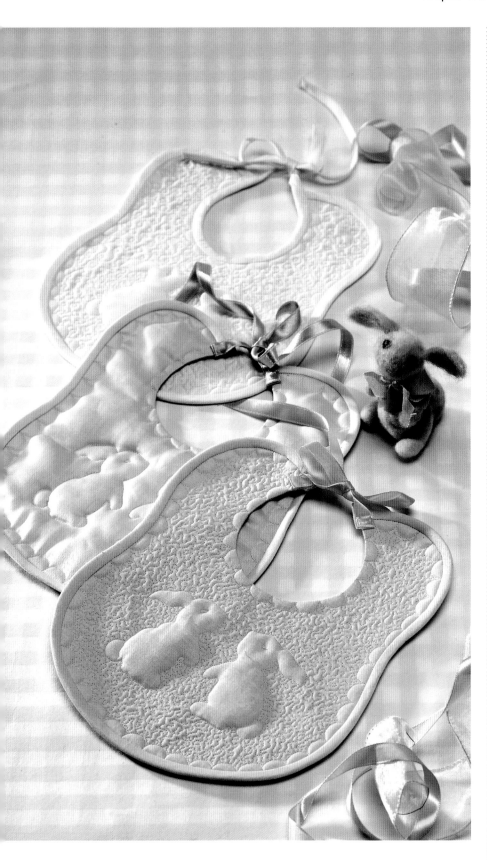

Alternative finishing technique

If you prefer, an additional piece of single-fold bias binding can be used to cover the neck opening and to make the ties.

1 Mark and layer the bib without stitching the neck opening first, then quilt as described in the main project.

2 Trim a scant $1/4$ in (6 mm) from the entire bib edge. Attach the binding around the outside edge first, turn, and stitch. Use a $1/4$-in (6-mm) seam allowance to attach 30 in (76 cm) of binding to the neck opening, centering the piece in the opening and leaving a tail at each end. Turn the binding over the opening, fold the raw edge under by $1/4$ in (6 mm), and pin on the back—as you did for the outer edge of the main bib project. Fold the tails in the same way and stitch the binding along the edge of the neck opening.

CHAPTER 5
Quilting designs
By Luise Roberts

You can spend a lifetime looking for the perfect design presented in the way you wish to use it. These motifs demonstrate how an image can be edited, manipulated, and adapted to your own needs, so that you can create the pattern you want from what you have. Have fun and be inspired.

Each page features one motif and a series of smaller illustrations showing just a few of the ways in which it could be used. In addition to rotating and reflecting an image, don't forget that a whole motif or selected areas can be distorted, simplified, or combined with other motifs to suit your needs. The main motif is 4 in (10 cm) square and can be enlarged by 150% to create a 6-in (15-cm) square block, or by 200% to create an 8-in (20-cm) square block. Start by copying the motif several times, then cut them out and place them until you have a design you are pleased with.

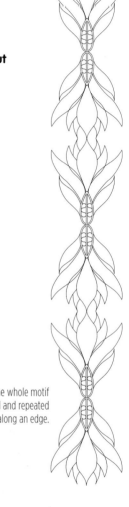

This motif could represent a fan of leaves with a pod at its base—remember, the components can be used separately or together.

The whole motif rotated and repeated along an edge.

The whole motif repeated and rotated through 90 degrees so the pods just touch.

A motif with the pod detail removed, repeated, and rotated through 72 degrees so the bases just touch.

The center five leaves repeated and rotated through 72 degrees so the leaves just touch.

This motif could represent a bramble, peony, or chrysanthemum—change the leaf detail to suit the rest of the motif.

A partial motif repeated along an edge.

A partial motif reflected and repeated along an edge.

The whole motif repeated and rotated through 90 degrees so the bases just touch.

Part of the main image isolated from the leaves.

A construction detail of the image to the left.

A basic motif of radiating spokes is always effective as a base for your own designs.

A partial motif reflected and repeated along an edge.

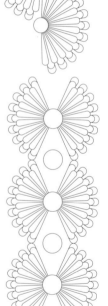

A partial motif reflected and repeated along an edge.

A simplified version of the main motif for smaller areas.

Even small alterations can make a big difference to the look of the motif.

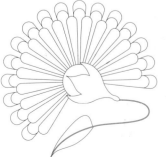

A partial motif combined with a leaf and calyx from the motif on page 117.

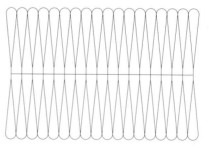

Part of the motif reflected and repeated along an edge.

A leaf or heart motif is an essential in any basic library.

A partial motif repeated along an edge.

A partial motif overlapped and repeated vertically along an edge.

A partial motif overlapped and repeated horizontally along an edge.

The motif repeated and rotated through 45 degrees so the bases just touch.

The motif reflected and repeated along a line.

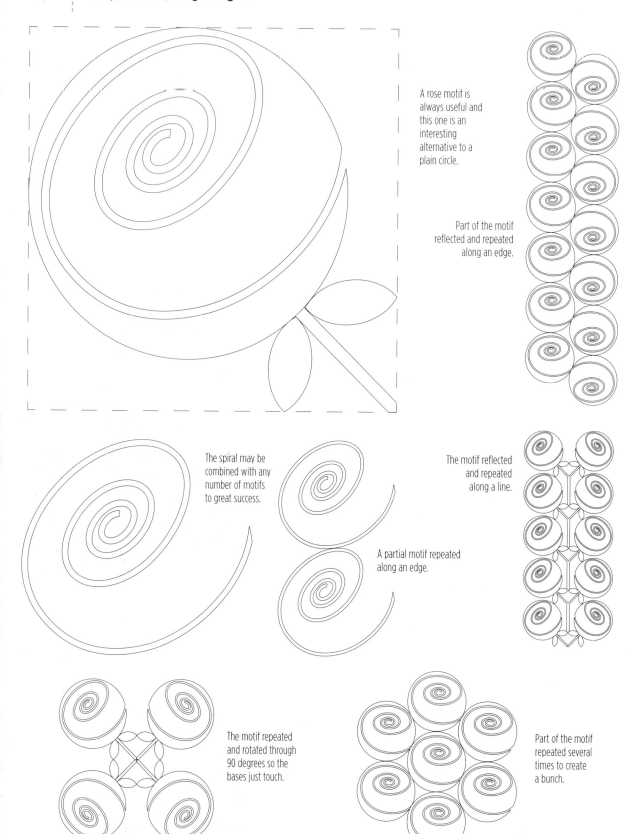

A rose motif is always useful and this one is an interesting alternative to a plain circle.

Part of the motif reflected and repeated along an edge.

The spiral may be combined with any number of motifs to great success.

The motif reflected and repeated along a line.

A partial motif repeated along an edge.

The motif repeated and rotated through 90 degrees so the bases just touch.

Part of the motif repeated several times to create a bunch.

Stylized bird motifs can be used to add movement to a quilt design. Nearly any motif or shape can be repeated to create a pair of wings.

The main motif has been combined with part of the motif on page 118 to create a bird with a fanned-out tail.

A pair of birds is a classic motif for the center of a border.

Simply change the beak or head to create a motif that is evocative of the bird of your choice. Look at stylized wooden folk carvings of birds for inspiration.

The main motif has been adapted and two hearts from page 119 used for each wing.

This shape does not really need a template. Use part of the circumference of a plate or cup to create the same shape.

The whole motif repeated and overlapped along an edge.

The motif repeated and rotated through 45 degrees so the bases just touch.

The motif reflected and repeated along an edge.

An edited version of the pattern to the left.

The motif repeated and rotated through 90 degrees around its center.

The main motif has been manipulated to create a different petal motif.

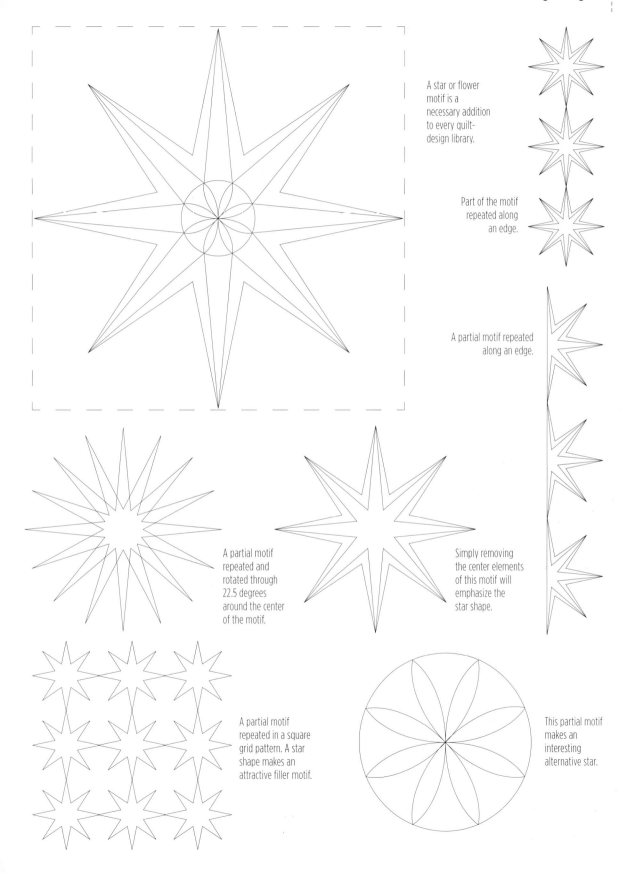

A star or flower motif is a necessary addition to every quilt-design library.

Part of the motif repeated along an edge.

A partial motif repeated along an edge.

A partial motif repeated and rotated through 22.5 degrees around the center of the motif.

Simply removing the center elements of this motif will emphasize the star shape.

A partial motif repeated in a square grid pattern. A star shape makes an attractive filler motif.

This partial motif makes an interesting alternative star.

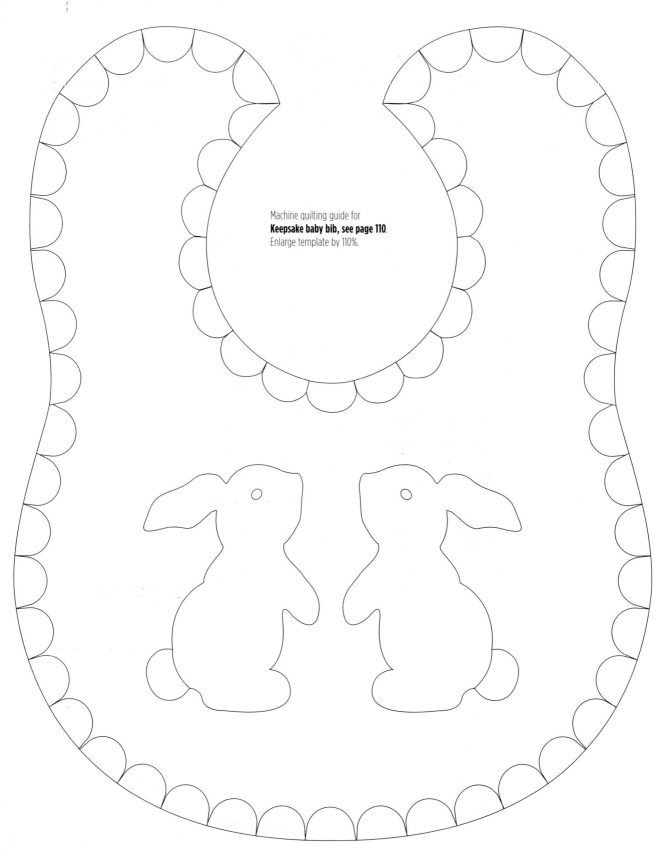

Machine quilting guide for
Keepsake baby bib, see page 110.
Enlarge template by 110%.

Machine quilting guide for **Toile bed quilt, see page 106**. This shows a quarter of the design; enlarge by 200%, then 200%, then 200%. Tape the pattern pieces together. Rotate the quarter guide to make one complete design. The curved edge in red shows the layout for the serpentine quilt edge.

Flap template for **Sewing tool caddy, see page 98**. Enlarge by 150%.

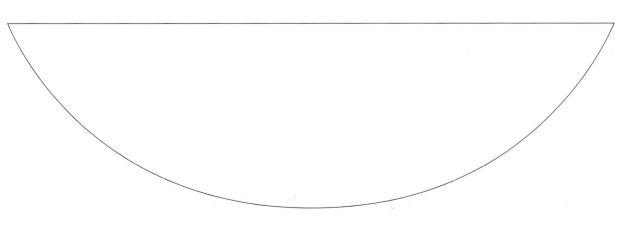

Index

Credits

Quarto would like to thank the following quilters for supplying images for inclusion in this book:

C. June Barnes, www.cjunebarnes.co.uk, p.9
Carole Sedgley, www.butterflyquilters.co.uk, p.78
Elizabeth Barton, http://ebarton.myweb.uga.edu, p.10
Ellin Larimer, www.ellinlarimer.com, p.12, 14, 79
Jeanette Meyer, www.jdmeyer.com, p.92
Jeri Riggs, http://jeririggs.com, p.15, 46b
Joanie Zeier Poole, http://heirloomquiltingdesigns.com, p.32, 33, 37, 44, 46t, 47, 48, 58, 63, 91t
Laura Glass, http://www.etsy.com/shop/LauraGlassArtQuilts, p.71
Loris Bogue, www.lorisbogue.com, p.80
Marijke de Boer-Boon, http://quiltpage.homestead.com, p.11, 93
Pam Levenhagen, p.48
Sally Bramald, http://quiltfeather.blogspot.com, p.8, 84
Sheena J. Norquay, http://sites.google.com/site/sheenajnorquay, p.13, 42

With special thanks to Bernina whose sewing machines are used in many of the sequences featured in these pages.

We would also like to thank the following manufacturers for supplying images:

Bernina www.bernina.co.uk;
Cotton Patch www.cottonpatch.co.uk;
Handi Quilter www.handiquilter.com;
The Grace Company www.graceframe.com.

Thanks to Jennifer Barlow, who assisted with step photography, and to Luise Roberts and Susan Briscoe for technical edits.

The book featured on page 36 is *1000 Motifs for Crafters* by Alan D. Gear and Barry L. Freestone, published by Collins & Brown.

All step-by-step and other images are the copyright of Quarto Publishing plc. While every effort has been made to credit contributors, Quarto would like to apologize should there have been any omissions or errors—and would be pleased to make the appropriate correction for future editions of the book.